FROM THE DESK OF

FROM THE DESK OF

BY

HAL DRUCKER AND SID LERNER
WITH F.P. MODEL · PHOTOGRAPHS BY SING-SI SCHWARTZ
WITH A FOREWORD BY STUDS TERKEL

HARCOURT BRACE JOVANOVICH, PUBLISHERS

San Diego   New York   London

Library of Congress Cataloging-in-Publication Data
Lerner, Sid.
From the desk of/Sid Lerner and Hal Drucker,
with F. P. Model; photographs by Sing-Si Schwartz;
with a foreword by Studs Terkel. — 1st ed.
p.   cm.
ISBN 0-15-133795-0
1. United States—Biography—Portraits.
2. Celebrities—United States—Portraits.
3. Biography—20th century—Portraits.
4. Desks—United States—Anecdotes.
I. Drucker, Hal. II. Model, F. Peter. III. Title.
CT120.L38   1989
920.073—dc20
[B]   89-37314

Printed in the United States of America
First edition
A B C D E

For Alice and Helaine

Photographer's Note

The portraits in this book were taken
with either a Hasselblad ELM or 500
CM, 2¼″ × 2¼″ camera. An assortment
of Hasselblad lenses, ranging in focal
lengths from 30mm to 120mm were
used, depending on the size of desk and
its location. Dynalite strobe equipment
and, on occasion, Speedotron power
packs, heads, and reflectors were used
for lighting. Chimera soft boxes and
Blacar grids were used to duplicate and
enhance the location's natural
environment. Eastman Kodak's E-6
Ektachrome 100 Plus film was used
because of its superior color saturation,
exposure latitude, contrast, and fine
grain structure. Polaroid film types 54,
55, and 59 were used to aid in
composition and exposure. Duggal
Color Projects, New York City, did the
color processing.

ACKNOWLEDGMENTS

The authors are grateful to Daphne Merkin for her vision, and for the advice, contributions, and assistance of:
Dan Abramson, Ed Arrendell, Robert Batcheler, Linda Becker, Louis Botto, Martin Bressler, Michael D. Brockman, The Brooklyn Museum, Mike Buckley, Major Napoleon B. Byars, Valerie Caccia, Monica Caulfield, Christie's East, Rosemary Connors, Larry Cooper, Jim Curry, Jr., Holly Dando, Danielle De Mers, E. Dan Dobson, Roger Dow, Alice Drucker, Baldev Duggal, Mary Elmore, Margo Feiden, Maureen Fitzpatrick, Norma Flynn, Jonathan Fox, Michael Frank, Cye Friedman, Diane Galante, Debbie Garrison, Caleb Gray, George Grey, Tracy Gulbenkian, Vernon Hammond, Charles J. Harbin III, Lillian Janklow, Bryan Kaatzis, Diana Kan, Rob Kearney, Maura Kelly, Randeep Khanna, Barbara Khoury, Karla Kurz, Jerrold H. Kushnick, Malcolm Labatt-Simon, Laura Leeds, Helaine Lerner, Sydney Lewis, Gregg McCarthy, Kate McGrath, Ed Maurer, Dorothy Morris, Kevin Nagle, Susan Namest, Samuel R. Newborn, Michael Nolan, Frank Olson, Rubin Pfeffer, Agnes Pilot, Val Pinchbeck, Pat Piper, Jamie Rasin, Connie Ridge, Beverly Robinson, Ann Rubin, Paul Schwartz, Claire Segal, Maurice Segal, Larry Shainman, Shazi Sheikh, Joan Shulman, Jerry Sloan, Erica Spaberg, George Speerin, Jeffrey Stone, Jill Strickman, Judy Thomas, Jeff Torres, William Truslow, Judy Tucker, Claire Wachtel, Marcia Wall, Paul Weisenstein, Terrie Williams, Shannon Wilkinson, and Sophia Xixis.

CONTENTS

FOREWORD

My first desk was a little desk. It had a little chair that was attached to it. It was at the McClaren School here in Chicago on the West Side, just half a block away from the rooming house in which we lived. I sat up front with all the short kids. The inkwell was recessed on the right side. My pen had a removable nib that you first had to wet with your lips before you dipped it in the inkwell. I was very slovenly. The ink would get under my fingers. It was tough to write your homework assignment on a desktop that resembled the surface of the moon as the result of years of knife markings from the scribes of the second grade. Did I add my initials? No, I was a good boy.

What I most remember, though, was not *my* desk but the desk of the man who owned the hotel where we leased rooms.

His name was Henry L. Flentye, and he was a great man—a workingman's workingman. He was an old McKinley Republican, a man of remarkable integrity and fairness. And he had a rrrrrrolltop desk. I remember that desk so well, that rolltop. He'd be writing out all those leases in longhand, with one of those fastidious Palmer penmanship flairs. I wrote a piece about my memory of those times and that wonderful old rolltop. And recently someone called up and told me he had that desk. If I wanted it I could have it. If I ever find a place to put it, I most certainly will proudly sit at the desk of Henry L. Flentye.

Of course, they hid Earl Williams the escaped convict in a rolltop desk. That is, Mr. Hecht and Mr. MacArthur did so in their play *The Front Page*. They modeled him after an actual escaped convict, Tommy O'Connor, who never was caught.

Another famous desk was the FDR desk, with all those interesting items, from Mickey Mouse to a miniature Fala. Can't you just see Mr. Roosevelt behind that desk, with that tilted cigarette holder, that insouciant air, and that great grin?

Thomas Wolfe had a stand-up desk of sorts. Actually he used the top of his icebox as a writing surface and studiously avoided raiding its contents. That's one way of avoiding writer's cramp.

Now my desk is a higgledy-piggledy desk. It's disheveled, disheveled as I am in my clothing. I am consistent in what I suppose you would call "dishevelry." It's not something deliberate. I'm just organically so. "Organic" was the favorite word of Frank Lloyd Wright. He said buildings should be as organic as the fingers on our hand. Organic dishevelry. That's how I work, and that's what I am.

Notice that the name of this book is *From the Desk Of:*—not simply *From:*

Today we have an accountability gap in our society. It's no longer Joe Doakes who's fielding the problem—it's the desk of Joe Doakes. When in doubt, put the blame on the desk. That wasn't Henry Flentye's way—nor is it the way of the forty-three good working people who grace the pages of this book.

Their desks and the things on them may tell you a lot more about these people and their work styles than a library of *Who's Who*s.

STUDS TERKEL

INTRODUCTION

Edward R. Murrow at his stand-up desk

T he simple relationship between man and desk is inescapable. The fourteenth-century Middle English word *deske*, a modification of the Old Italian *desco* (table), was derived from the Latin *discus* (dish, disk), which the Romans in turn plagiarized from the Greek *discos* (a form of the verb *dikein*, to throw).

If we are to believe our etymology, Petrarch wrote his sonnets on a table, Plautus his plays on a dinner plate, and Plato his *Republic* on an early Frisbee. The Etruscans, Egyptians, and Sumerians must all have written on something, put their feet up on something, filled out their tax forms on something. From Cro-Magnon times, desks, or various primordial predecessors, afforded an irresistible form of personal expression.

The desk, where persiflage is penned and music is composed, drawings are drawn and ideas

conceived, has the uncanny ability of assuming the demeanor of whoever sits, struts, or frets his hours behind it. And no amount of careful design or costly expenditure can overshadow the sense of place, invincibility, truth, and power a desk inevitably conveys.

The regal presidential desk crafted from the sturdy teak timbers of the H.M.S. *Resolute* and presented in 1878 to Rutherford B. Hayes by Queen Victoria tells us one thing about John F. Kennedy and quite another about George Bush.

The public persona of Edward R. Murrow as a comfortably settled, pinstriped, chain-smoking *Person to Person* interviewer in a deep-back lounge chair is at odds with the actuality of the kinetic newsman who favored a stand-up desk.

Kennedy Kids, at his desk

In these pages, forty-three of America's most influential and admired men and women are seen as they seldom are: captured by photographer Sing-Si Schwartz in an unexpected and illuminating light, at their individual command posts, among the artifacts of their working lives.

For those whose work demands solitude—writers like Gail Sheehy, William Safire, Neil Simon, and Studs Terkel; composer/performers like André Previn, Sammy Cahn, and Wynton Marsalis; visual artists like Al Hirschfeld, Cathy Guisewite, Frank Gehry, John Weitz, Geoffrey Holder, and Yoko Ono—the desk (even when it takes the form of an easel or a piano) becomes an intimate reflection of work habits, taste, and personality, enhancing the creative process.

What are we to make of comedian Jay Leno, whose desk is in his garage; of movie critic Roger Ebert, whose desk is a cross between Fantasyland and *War of the Worlds*; of actress Stockard Channing, whose desk doubles as a kitchen table; of cookie queen Debbi Fields, whose desk adjoins a miniature day-care center; of producers Simpson and Bruckheimer, whose desk is a candidate for the *Guinness Book of Records*; or of sportscaster John Madden, whose desk rides on a moving object?

And what of the desk strewn with unlit cigars, pastramis-on-rye, or fossils (see Terkel, Dershowitz, Gould) vs. the pristine desktops of a Justice Brennan or a Barbara Walters?

What is hidden in Bill Safire's rolltop; what are the surprising desk accessories of Jackie Joyner-Kersee, Betsey Johnson, or Larry King; why isn't Julia Child's desk in the kitchen, and how does Alistair Cooke speak to George Shearing?

How about that baseball cap on the desk of Senator Nancy Kassebaum, those teeth on the desk of Lars-Eric Lindblad, the walking cake on screen director John Carpenter's desk, that seagull with an embedded baseball near Dave Winfield's desk, and those fascinating photos on the desks of Douglas Fairbanks, Jr., and Princess Yasmin Aga Khan?

Then there are those who play the high-stakes power-desk games: CEOs Petersen, Marriott, Della Femina, and Bing; Joint Chiefs of Staff Chairman Crowe (the man of a thousand hats); Mayor Ed Koch (standing behind a piece of New York history destined for his City Hall successors). Their success or popularity may well hinge on their ability to exploit the expressive potency of their desks.

From the Desk Of: provides us with rare insights into the complexities, ambiguities, and ironies of the men and women for whom the desk is—for better or worse—their altar ego.

Bush at Oval Office desk

PRINCESS YASMIN AGA KHAN

Princess Yasmin Aga Khan is a tireless fundraiser and spokesperson for the Alzheimer's Association.

At first glimpse, there is no question that she is the epitome of Glamour with a capital *G*, a favorite of society-page editors and columnists on both sides of the Atlantic—and why not? As the daughter of two of the most Beautiful People in recent history—film goddess Rita Hayworth and *bon vivant* Prince Aly Khan, stepbrother of Aga Khan IV, the spiritual leader of fifteen million Moslems—and as the granddaughter of His Highness Mohammed Sultan Shah Aga Khan, Princess Yasmin makes news just by Being There.

In spite of her Los Angeles/ Geneva/Cannes/New England upbringing—and her not insignificant lineage—she has a solidly anchored "real-life" existence.

Most people recall that film goddess Rita Hayworth died of Alzheimer's Disease. What few know is that her daughter personally cared for her during the debilitating course of the terrible illness, giving up her hopes of pursuing an operatic career (a three-octave light mezzo, the princess graduated in 1973 from Bennington College as a music major). Through this agonizing period—"I believe very strongly in the family unit"—she became an authority on the illness.

Today Princess Yasmin is a chief spokesperson and driving force behind the Alzheimer's Disease and Related Disorders Association. She serves on the national board of directors as vice-chairman. "When I began caring for my mother," she says, "nobody had ever heard of Alzheimer's Disease. There were just a handful of us at first, back in 1980, trying to raise enough money for our first simple computer. Starting with a budget of $80,000, we have grown to an organization that has distributed over $10 million in research grants. Today there are 190 Alzheimer's Association chapters and over 1,200 support groups throughout the United States."

She and an assistant work from an office in her Central Park West Manhattan apartment, fully equipped with all the necessary professional accoutrements—fax machine, word processor, seven-line telephone. In the entranceway, to the left of Yasmin's work space, is a photograph of her mother that was colorized by German artist Art Rimmfer, an admirer of her performances in *Blood and Sand*, *Cover Girl*, *Pal Joey*, and her memorable "Put the Blame on Mame" number in *Gilda*. Directly over the desk is a floral oil painted by the screen siren in 1956. In the dining area to the right hangs an imposing Scavullo portrait of Hayworth.

Three bulging Rolodexes dominate Yasmin's inlaid English desk. "I'd be lost without them," she admits. Also on the desk is a large framed photograph of her stepgrandmother, Begum Mohammed Sultan Shah Aga Khan. The princess speaks weekly to her grandmother, who now lives in Switzerland. There are assorted photos of her three-year-old son, Andrew, and her husband, real estate executive Christopher Jeffries (taken at the 1987 Deauville Film Festival's *hommage à Hayworth*). "He's the love of my life, next to Andrew."

Much of Yasmin's time is occupied in planning benefits throughout the country, which have raised over three million dollars for the Alzheimer's Association since 1984. "We've had four galas here in New York, two in Chicago, and one in Dallas," she recalls. "People like Douglas Fairbanks, Jr., Anthony Quinn, Willard Scott, Angie Dickinson, Britt Ekland, and Robin Leach have been tremendously helpful."

Between the phone and additional Alzheimer's materials are a Tiffany clock, awarded to Yasmin in 1985 by the Alzheimer's Association to commemorate her distinguished leadership; a 1987 photograph of her with President Reagan in the Oval Office, at his signing of the "National Alzheimer's Awareness Month" proclamation; two decorative crystal paperweights; and Veenie, her opulent cat, which she adopted from an ASPCA office fourteen years ago.

"We're together for life," says Princess Yasmin.

FROM THE DESK OF:

DAVE BING

The night the
Pistons retired
Bing's number
21

March 18, 1983 | BING 21

PICSONIC PRODUCTIONS

The onetime Syracuse University All-American hoopster and Detroit Pistons all-everything shooting guard—Dave Bing—is starring in his personal Act Two as CEO of Bing Steel Co., a rolled-steel-manufacturer Bing founded in 1980, which now employs seventy workers and does business in seven states.

Bing Steel occupies a block-long two-story industrial office and warehouse building in central Detroit. The team's key player works out of a second-floor office, above the first-floor employee lunchroom, garage, and storage areas. On the upper level are more executive offices and a wide range of business machines.

Bing's spare and modern office is a mini-museum of sports mementos, action and ceremonial photos, and family snapshots going back to his early playing days at Springarn High School in Washington, D.C. His college stardom was something of a break in tradition for Syracuse, which had been on a roll for its succession of such football stars as Jim Brown, Ernie Davis, John Mackey, Larry Csonka, and Floyd Little. Bing graduated in 1966, with a B.A. in marketing. His collegiate roommate, Jim Boeheim, is now SU's successful basketball coach. A favorite oncourt college and pro rival was Bill Bradley, who is now a U.S. senator from New Jersey and still a close friend.

Near the desk are photos of Bing with former President Reagan and Michigan Governor Jim Blanchard, receiving awards from the Rotary Club, the Black United Fund, and the YMCA of Detroit. "Being involved in the community was never a second thought, because where I was raised, we were taught to remember where we had come from." Bing works with SHAR (Self Help Addiction Rehabilitation) and has spent time talking with recovering addicts about how, as a young NBA star fresh out of college, he confronted the pressures on the road without resorting to drugs. He has also worked on a number of community service projects in tandem with Detroit Mayor Coleman A. Young.

On the wall is a framed certificate commemorating Bing's number 21, retired by the Pistons on March 18, 1983, the only such honor in the history of the franchise. He was named to the NBA All-Star team seven times and won the league scoring title. Bing played for the Washington Bullets and the Boston Celtics before exiting from pro basketball in 1978. During his professional off seasons, he was a management trainee for the National Bank of Detroit and later for Chrysler Corporation, preparation for his current role.

Supporting players include Bing's three daughters (photos on top bookcase): Cassaundra and Bridgett, Michigan State grads, both of whom work at Bing Steel, and Aleisha, a Syracuse sophomore.

The bookcase also features an eight-track Emerson Multiplex sound unit, with turntable, cassette player, and AM/FM options. It is invariably tuned to jazz recordings and local station WJZZ.

Center court in the office is the businesslike oak pedestal desk, which carries a daily agenda and correspondence, plus an appointment book and business portfolio. A pair of corporate pens are kept in the "down" position in their setting. There is also a 1984 Detroit World Championship Award—souvenir of Dave's brief career as a sports announcer—and a sign that reads "Thank you for not smoking."

Behind Bing's desk, a basketball on a short pedestal is inscribed: "Eighteen thousandth point in the National Basketball Association—Cleveland, 9/18/78." An apothecary jar is filled with mints, which are offered to visitors. Employees keep the jar filled "as an excuse to come in here and talk to me."

Too bad F. Scott Fitzgerald didn't live long enough to meet Dave Bing. Had he watched him in action, he'd never have written: "There are no second acts in American lives."

JUSTICE WILLIAM J. BRENNAN

Justice Brennan, fourth from the left, has 32 years on the bench.

ART LIEN, NBC NEWS

In the case of Supreme Court Justice William Joseph Brennan, Jr.—at eighty-three the high tribunal's oldest, most liberal, and, according to most of the clerks, warmest and friendliest member—the man clearly makes the office. In a town where the *trappings* of power sometime take on an excessively disproportionate importance, Brennan's plain and simple working environment is totally unpretentious.

The diminutive Irishman, a former labor lawyer (Harvard Law, '31) who came to the U.S. Supreme Court by way of the New Jersey Supreme Court, arrived in Washington thirty-two years ago to fill the vacancy created by the death of Justice Sherman Minton. He has never stood on ceremony. In fact, when he moved into these chambers, he made only one change: he replaced Minton's desk with the one last occupied

by his idol, Justice Louis Brandeis (1916–39). The gleaming partners desk is barren of personal doodads (save for a small framed photo of Brennan's second wife, Mary, his personal secretary of twenty-six years, whom he married in 1983). There are two phones; one faces the visitor's chair and is presumably for use by a fellow justice: It is directly connected to the eight other suites.

On the windowsill, next to a miniature American flag engraved with the Pledge of Allegiance, is a pedestal supporting a miniature bust of JFK by sculptor Robert Berk. It is the sole clue to Brennan's political inclination. The high-ceilinged, thickly carpeted, oak-paneled room, redolent of wood polish and burnished leather, could easily be that of any high-level government department head instead of the sanctum sanctorum where Brennan—heir to

William O. Douglas's mantle—wrote such landmark majority opinions as *Baker* v. *Carr* (reapportionment) and *New York Times* v. *Sullivan* (free speech).

The only articles attesting to the occupant's calling might be the full set of *U.S. Law Reports*, spilling over into two bookcases; a large framed reproduction of the Bill of Rights; and (not shown) two framed documents—Brennan's recess appointment by President Dwight D. Eisenhower and his congressional appointment six months later.

Brennan, an early riser, arrives hours before the Court convenes at 10:00 A.M., usually lunches at his desk, and puts in a long day. He has been described as the high court's "most likable and politically adept coalition builder," a "master of patience and guile [whose] easy smile and twinkling blue eyes . . . give him a leprechaun's appearance." That he offers no argument to that is suggested by the green felt pixie hat, complete with orange feather, sitting atop one of the room's two mantelpieces—an eightieth-birthday gift from one of his four law clerks. Another evidence of Brennan's good humor hangs, somewhat incongruously, off one of the wood-paneled walls: the popular poster "A New Jerseyan's View of the World" in the style of Saul Steinberg's famous *New Yorker* cover.

The child in the large pencil sketch over the fireplace is his daughter Nancy, drawn by one of his sons' wives at the time of his appointment. "Nancy," he proudly adds, "is now forty and is the director of Baltimore's city museums, including the Peale Museum."

Nowhere does the *essential* Brennan come through more clearly than in the family pictures that seem to occupy every spare inch of shelf, bookcase, and mantel space. Most of the subjects are his children, grandchildren, and great-grandchildren, many wearing the "official" family sweatshirt, stenciled *Brennan's Brigade.*

FROM THE DESK OF:

HELEN GURLEY BROWN

Since July 1965, Helen Gurley Brown's *Cosmo* has been burning up the newsstands.

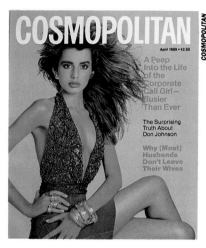

"**M**ine is the *dullest* desk in the world," declaims *Cosmopolitan* Girl Helen Gurley Brown. "There isn't a *thing* on it you would possibly want to talk about."

Well, maybe not. The desk is a three-drawered, Louis XIV–style *bureau plat* reproduction. Other than the basket of fresh-cut flowers, little distinguishes this desktop from countless others, with its in and out boxes, memo pad holder, paper clip container (an imitation Ainsley bone china rice bowl), and Toby mug containing an American flag. A Tiffany captain's clock, a thirty-four-station phone console, a pile of manuscripts, and an appointment book cover the remaining leather-topped surface.

But certainly worth discussing is why she persists on banging away on a vintage Royal manual typewriter when everyone else

at *Cosmo* is on word processors; and why her eighth-floor office in the Hearst Magazine Building, on New York's West Fifty-seventh Street, doesn't look like the lair of one of the nation's most powerful magazine editors, who also happens to show up, year after year, on the *World Almanac*'s list of "The 25 Most Influential Women in the U.S."

Like the sprawling co-op apartment thirty blocks uptown she shares with her husband of thirty years—former Zanuck/Brown producer David Brown (*Jaws*, *The Sting*, *Cocoon*), who has just started a new company—her office is comfortable without being ostentatious. The rare magazine editor who still *writes*, she thrives in clutter, professing to abhor the pristine office look favored by some of her nonwriting peers "over on the east side of town."

That this is the ultimate office/den is obvious from the

abundance of mirrors and potted plants, the floral-patterned wallpaper and the matching couch with its maxim-stitched "fun pillows," the myriad novelty-framed photographs and the knickknacks scattered on the wraparound credenza.

Just a few of Mrs. Brown's collections that contribute to the cozy femininity of this atypical editor-in-chief's office are her antique porcelain dolls and the framed Victorian postcards—"not French!"—titled "Great Moments in a Girl's Life."

She also has a knack for collecting people. On her "photo wall" is a plush, heart-shaped framed shot of herself with a dozen staffers taken seven years ago at her sixtieth-birthday party. She's pleased to say that nine of the twelve are still with her at the magazine.

Cosmo's official biography describes the schoolteachers' daughter from Little Rock as a "non-militant feminist," which she laughingly translates as "an irredeemable but contented workaholic, just like the boys, with one exception: I want fresh flowers on my desk in the morning."

Hearst is more than happy to pay the bill. They should be. In 1965—three years after writing *Sex and the Single Girl*, which, in sixteen languages published in twenty-eight countries, said it

was OK for single women over forty to both want and get it all—she gave up advertising copywriting to take on the ailing *Cosmopolitan* magazine, which Hearst was about to fold. She turned it into a veritable advertising gold mine as one of America's top five newsstand magazines, with a circulation of just under three million and fifteen overseas editions.

Here's one book you have no trouble telling from its cover. *Advertising Age* once declared: "If the glamour does not get you, the double-barreled blast of cover-lines will, detailing saucy secrets to love and life in a *Cosmo* world." From the very first issue overseen by Brown, those compelling, frequently torrid lines have sprung from the fertile mind of showman/helpmate David Brown who, despite his own frenetic globe-trotting schedule, always delivers on time.

How did the *Cosmo* Girl evolve? "I felt I knew what she should be like from the very first issue," says Brown. "Sexy, gorgeous, friendly—someone you'd like to talk to as well as look at."

FROM THE DESK OF:

SAMMY CAHN

"It's unusual for me to pose like this at my desk," insists lyricist Sammy Cahn, seventy-six, "because I usually start writing the minute I sit down." Whereupon Cahn turned his back to photographer Sing-Si Schwartz and promptly pecked out:

I oughta be in pictures
I know that sounds grotesque
I oughta be in pictures
And for a book called
From the Desk.

The book has lots of mixtures
From Art right to Burlesk
I oughta be in pictures
There in a book called
From the Desk.

Long regarded by his peers as the most facile of musical wordsmiths, Cahn spins out lyrics on demand in as little as fifteen minutes for such friends as the charter members of the "Bev-erly Hills Rat Pack"—Frank Sinatra, Dean Martin, and Sammy Davis, Jr. Let others say they are bi-coastal; Sammy Cahn boasts he's "bi-deskal," his matching IBM Executive typewriters filled with oversized capital letters. He once explained his method to Prince Charles: "I just put my fingers on the keyboard and walk away."

Sammy's functional Manhattan desk sports a framed *New York Times* crossword puzzle (June 18, 1984), in which editor Eugene Maleska buried his name and three of his song titles. Perched on a porcupine-quill box crammed with trivia are photos of his son and daughter, his grandchildren, and his wife, Tita (who bought him the three-camel pewter lamp). The piano music box chimes out "My Kind of Town (Chicago Is)" when Cahn lifts the lid. "And every time I do," says Cahn mischievously, "I get a royalty."

Partnered with composer Jule Styne, he wrote the 1947 Broadway musical *High Button Shoes*, which starred Phil Silvers and Nanette Fabray (framed *Playbill* mounted above desk, left). With Styne and Jimmy Van Heusen, he wrote four Oscar-winning movie songs: "Three Coins in the Fountain," "All the Way," "High Hopes," and "Call Me Irresponsible." Since 1974, he has been president of the Songwriters Hall of Fame.

Born Sammy Cohen on Manhattan's Lower East Side, he started out in burlesque, writing custom lyrics for strippers and jugglers. "I first scored—pardon the pun—in 1938, when I wrote 'Bei Mir Bist du Schoen' for the Andrews Sisters." Speedwriting for Glen Gray's Casa Loma Band and the Tommy Dorsey Orchestra, with such arrangers as Axel Stordahl and Paul Weston, he worked his way across the country and onto the lots of Republic, Columbia, Paramount, and Metro-Goldwyn-Mayer. It was at M-G-M that he took his present surname. "I kept being confused with a rising comic named Sammy Cohen, so I changed my name to Kahn, only to run into Gus Kahn, which explains the *C*."

Since 1974, Cahn has been touring the world with his one-man show, *Words and Music*, in which he reminds the audience that "my words obviously wouldn't 'sing' if it weren't for the singers."

When asked, inevitably, "What comes first, the words or the music?" he will respond, inCahntestably, "The phone call."

And when that phone rings, he doesn't bother with "Hello" or other trite pleasantries. "Here I am!" he'll say joyfully. Just call him irrepressible.

On location with Carpenter, who made his first film at eight, with his father's 8 mm camera

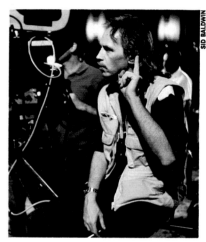

Even those who know John Carpenter to be America's premier *auteur* of the horror film—*Halloween, The Fog, The Thing, Escape from New York*, etc.—are apt to experience a jolt of the unexpected as they enter his inner sanctum, in a cottage behind his Los Angeles home. There, hovering over his IBM PC, is the fiercest of hawks, wings outstretched, beak quivering for the kill—but stuffed, of course. The predatory bird could double as Carpenter's product trademark: unpredictable and scary as hell. He himself may not be scary, but he surely is unpredictable. Asked whom he regards as his "all-time greatest heroes," Carpenter reels off three names (drumroll): Roman Polanski, Hulk Hogan, and John Wayne. On the desk the visitor notes the late Professor Richard Feynman's autobiography, and paraphrases its title by asking,

"Surely you're joking, Mr. Carpenter?" He replies, "You *bet!*"

In atypical Hollywood understatement, his official studio bio begins: "For years, the films of John Carpenter have jangled the nerves of movie audiences everywhere." He wanted to do so ever since he was five, when someone took him to see Ray Bradbury's *It Came from Outer Space*, the 3-D thriller made back in 1953, which is still a late-late-show standard. Not many five-year-olds make career path decisions, but Carpenter did. Within three years, he had learned to use his father's 8mm camera, and he spent countless hours at the movies. That he would major in cinematography at the University of Southern California was a foregone conclusion. While at USC, he produced *Dark Star*, which he describes as a "comic sci-fi film." It premiered at the 1974 Los Angeles Film Exposition and

probably led him, ten years later, to return to outer space with *Starman*, a warmly mocking morality tale about man's inhumanity to visiting ETs.

Four years after *Dark Star* came *Halloween*, a low-budget thriller about a psychotic child-killer, with lots of "in" jokes for fellow film buffs. At the time the most successful independent film ever made, *Halloween* begat *Halloween II*, et seq. Carpenter did the first sequel, then he let others clone the title—for hefty royalties—and looked the other way as they savaged the original story line. Carpenter also composes his own film music, using the steel-stringed guitar as others might use a piano.

The objects in his office and the books he reads tell a lot about the real John Carpenter. He's turned his work space into an approximation of an all-American den. There is nothing pretentious here. The desk is a custom-modeled, modestly scaled oak affair, kept pretty much clear of torture instruments. He does like to play with a wind-up novelty cake that slithers—his word—across the desk. Casually slipped in with such eclectic reading and reference matter as the Feynman bio, Dr. Stephen Hawking's *A Brief History of Time, The Synonym Finder*, and a thick volume on quantum mechanics (a subject that's fascinated him for the past

three years) are two anthologies he might regard as reference books: *Bloodcurdling Tales of Horror* and *Tales and Poems of Edgar Allan Poe*. The script of *They Live* lies on the desk, near the phone, along with two sets of eyeglasses—"in case 'They' spirit one set away when I'm not looking." These and a movie poster for *The Thing* on the far wall, along with framed photographs taken of friends on the sets of several of his movies—producer Sandy King, actor Dennis Dunn, producer Larry Franco—are the only visible clues to the primary interest of the room's occupant.

The only incongruous touch, to those who do not know John Carpenter, is the helicopter pilot's cap bearing the logo of Hamilton-Standard, a leading manufacturer of helicopter rotors. For Carpenter's idea of R and R is to drive out to Burbank, get into his Bell Long Ranger III helicopter, and do the long circuit: over the HOLLYWOOD sign, toward Santa Monica, then over the San Gabriel Mountains and back down again. "Afterwards, I'm just as peaceful as a . . . *hawk*."

STOCKARD CHANNING

A star of stage, TV, and film, Channing is a rare triple threat.

"Acting is a very strange, nomadic life," observes Stockard Channing, a native New Yorker who shuttles between homes in Manhattan, Los Angeles, and the Maine woods. While she loves to cook—her "desk" is actually a nineteenth-century cherrywood table smack-dab in the kitchen of her recently purchased Park Avenue co-op—she's got her priorities straight. "If the phone rings and I happen to be in the middle of a *soufflé*, I let it drop, and I'm out the door to catch the next plane."

As a Harvard student who majored in American history and literature, she managed to act in thirty-five plays—her first role being Jenny in a college production of Weill and Brecht's *The Threepenny Opera*—and after years of serving the obligatory apprenticeship, she made her professional Broadway debut as an understudy in a musical version of *Two Gentlemen from Verona*. She was featured in the film version of *Grease*. She has starred in Alan Ayckbourne's *Woman in Mind* (and won the coveted Drama Desk Award for Best Actress), Peter Nichols's *Joe Egg* (and won a Tony Award for Best Actress), and John Guare's *The House of Blue Leaves* at Lincoln Center (and was nominated for both awards). She's had her own TV sitcom series, been nominated for an Emmy for last year's dramatic miniseries *Echoes in the Darkness*, and won an ACE cable TV award for her performance in Harvey Fierstein's *Tidy Endings*.

Standing in the spacious kitchen of her new apartment, Channing says, "I told the agent I'd buy this place only if the owner threw in this chopping block—and I wasn't kidding, either." Her gourmet cook status is evidenced by the hanging pots, scattered cookbooks and restaurant guides, the "industrial-strength" six-burner, two-oven stove, and bottles of spices and what she euphemistically calls "homemade vinegars"— wines that have gone bad.

"During the renovation, I sat here and made lists and prayed that the workers would be out of here before I went crazy." It's her control center, where she often does "five things at once," including the reading of scripts that are constantly thrust before her. Behind the desk she's hung two large framed 1925 schoolroom maps—"the kind the teacher used to roll down over the blackboard during the geography lesson."

It would not be too farfetched to say that Stockard Channing "lives" in the kitchen. With its high ceilings, tiled floors—"the original owner had a home in Florence and actually brought in Italian workers to lay the tiles"—and airy cabinets amply stocked with long-stemmed champagne glasses, her kitchen-cum-office is a magnet for visitors. "When they come over, people head straight for it," she says.

Channing's phone is here—"I couldn't live without Call Waiting"—and the obligatory answering machine. She reads the *New York Times* on this table while drinking her morning coffee from an oversized French cup. "I write letters, make notes, keep my diaries." She even watches TV here.

"I have TVs in every room in this place," she admits cheerfully, "and watch constantly— especially Cable News Network . . . and I *love* the Weather Channel.

"You know what they say about New York: 'If you don't like the weather, wait a minute.'"

JULIA CHILD

ALFRED A. KNOPF, INC.

As the eponymous cooking instructor of PBS television's long-running *The French Chef*, she endeared herself to her millions of viewers as a harried housewife, ferociously wielding her giant balloon whisk, who kept offering sage advice to herself in Childian malapropisms. As the bifocals slipped, ingredients kerplopped to the floor. Yet she remained unflappable: "If this happens, just scoop it back. Remember, you are alone in the kitchen, and nobody can see you!"

Was it all an act? Could *that* tall but frazzled TV housewife be the same blue-eyed, brown-haired Julia Child who now sits—cool, unflustered, and *totally* in control of her environment—in an office directly above the kitchen Craig Claiborne once described as "the best-equipped in all of Boston"?

Yes, indeed. She regales the visitor with a rendering of how her written testimony brought down the House of Representatives last year. Along with other members of the Authors Guild, she lobbied Congress to throw out a provision in the 1986 Tax Reform Act that would have denied writers the right to deduct expenses in the year they were incurred. Mrs. Child wasted no time on emotional appeals; hers cut right to the bone of the matter when she asked, in effect: How does the IRS want writers like me to allocate the oregano? By the pinch? The argument reportedly got a round of applause; the committee got the point; and Julia got back her concurrent write-offs.

Kitchen and office occupy most of the first and second floors of the three-story clapboard house in Cambridge, Massachusetts, that Mr. and Mrs. Paul Cushing Child bought in 1961 upon his retirement.

Julia and Paul had met in 1943 in wartime Ceylon (now Sri Lanka), while both were in the OSS. She wanted to be a spy but settled for file clerk; he was an artist-turned-mapmaker, who liked good food. They went from India to Chungking and Kunming, China; got married after the war; moved in 1948 to Paris, where he worked for USIA and she took cooking lessons from a disciple of Auguste Escoffier. She formed a lasting friendship with Simone Beck and Louisette Bertholle, and the three women organized their own cooking school, L'Ecole des Trois Gourmandes (five dollars a lesson). Wherever the government sent the Childs—Marseilles, Bonn, Oslo —branches of L'Ecole were set up. A huge book began taking shape, which Alfred A. Knopf, an astute gourmet, snapped up. Published in 1961, *Mastering the Art of French Cooking* did not become a best-seller until Julia Child went on the air two years later, following a guest shot on a book-and-author show. WGBH-TV's Russell Morash, who would become her longtime producer-director, remembers asking himself, "Who *is* this madwoman, and *why* is she cooking an omelet on a book review show?" He soon found out, as viewers all over America reorganized their social lives around Monday nights at nine. The series changed forever the way America eats.

The French Chef and its se-quels have now run for an astounding twenty-five years. Though Julia Child hasn't been "live" for the past few years, producer Morash is now looking for funding to bring her back for a new PBS series. Meanwhile, she's not been idle. In between visits to the Childs' other homes, in Santa Barbara and the south of France, she pops up now and then on ABC's *Good Morning America*, and after four years of writing a column for *Parade*, she's just come out with a big illustrated how-to book based on those columns, *The Way to Cook*, which is supplemented by six hour-long teaching cassettes.

The Child house is a model of organization. The office, like the kitchen below, is laid out ergometrically so that everything, including computer *and* electric typewriter, is within easy reach—or roll of the swivel chair. With the window wall garnished by framed honors, diplomas, certificates, and personal photographs, the other three walls are lined with cookbooks—two thousand at last count—and squeezed in between desk and sundry tables are eighteen steel file drawers and ten cardboard storage files crammed with more recipes, categorized and subcategorized. "Cooking," Julia Child says, "is such a jolly profession. I've been cooking for more than forty years, and there's still so much to learn."

ADMIRAL WILLIAM J. CROWE, JR.

On his desk is the hat of his Russian counterpart, Marshal Sergei F. Akhromeyev.

With an ingenuousness that belies his rank and station as Chairman of the United States Joint Chiefs of Staff, Admiral William J. Crowe, Jr., sits jauntily on the edge of his desk.

The problem is, the most powerful peacetime military officer in the country's history rarely has a chance to take a breather. He marches promptly each day into his Pentagon office at 6:45 A.M. (followed by an entourage of senior staff officers), breakfasts at his desk, and immediately launches into a solid ten-to-twelve-hour workday, punctuated by a simple tray lunch and drafts of water from freshly filled thermoses.

His desktop, security-cleared for this photography session, is usually heaped with top-secret papers, which conceal the now visible statue of Neptune, a calculator, inscribed crystal plaques, a pen set, and a mounted spyglass given him by his British naval counterpart.

The scrambled-egg-braided hat of his Russian counterpart (Marshal Sergei F. Akhromeyev, since retired), perched on the desk's own right, is temporarily hidden in this photo by the avuncular "diplomat-warrior."

Ah, the hats: sombrero, cardinal's cap, campaign hat, fez, yarmulke, overseas cap, tricorner, ten-gallon, turban, Tyrolean, gondolier, kepi, American Indian headdress, Pacific Islands headdress, baseball cap, cricket cap, tam-o'-shanter, porkpie, borsalino, bobby's helmet, barrister's powdered wig, Prussian spiked helmet, Oklahoma Sooner football helmet . . .

The admiral didn't shop for the chapeaus; he received them as gifts. And each one reflects an experience or a relationship warm and solid enough to inspire the giving.

His collection of headgear originated in 1976 with a Down Under bush hat presented to him by the chief of staff of the Australian Army. Today hats overflow his office, assembled in serried ranks on his bookshelves and spilling over onto racks, chairs, and other surfaces. Over nine hundred head coverings are on display here and at a museum in Oklahoma City.

Crowe is not one to move along traditional routes, and his naval career path has been highly unorthodox. In the "onward and upward" department, he's figuratively sailed from the crest of one career crisis to that of the next—a record many of his Navy associates felt was more appropriate to early retirement than to promotion.

In 1962, the Navy selected Commander Crowe for its nuclear submarine program, but he elected instead to enter Princeton and work toward a Ph.D. in political science. His father had been a strong proponent of graduate education, a factor that influenced the son's decision to risk the wrath of the Navy establishment.

Three years later, after completing his degree, he returned to duty a changed man. He now realized that there was more to the world than the Navy. He had become flexible, ready to question. And he was a facile negotiator. The Navy assigned him to political affairs posts at the Pentagon and, in Vietnam, to commands usually shunned by fellow officers.

Crowe's appointment as Joint Chiefs Chairman was actually the product of a series of one-thing-leads-to-another coincidences. His selection as Chairman and reconfirmation for a second term was clearly abetted by the fact that while at Princeton, Admiral Crowe learned "how to think outside the Navy context," recognizing the importance of interservice cooperation. This perspective helped generate enthusiastic support among the members of the other military services.

Asked what keeps him going in the face of his formidable responsibilities, the man who appeared as himself in the sitcom *Cheers* indicates that his sense of humor helps immensely. As he puts it, "There's no situation without its ludicrous side. Even failure. To understand that simple reality is probably the first sign of maturity."

His heroes? General Robert E. Lee and Kemal Ataturk are two: the former because he could recover from his mistakes and forge ahead; the latter because of his ability to win, despite pitifully limited resources.

Whom does he envy? Those who don't agonize constantly over face-the-music decisions. He cites the astronaut Gordon Cooper, who fell asleep in the capsule awaiting lift-off. Says Admiral Crowe, "Now that's real class. When he blasted off, his pulse went to seventy. Mine," he continues, "hits ninety just *thinking* about it."

JERRY DELLA FEMINA

What appealed most to young Della Femina about advertising was that the people sat with "their feet up on their desks."

In his starkly modern penthouse office in a converted printing plant in lower Manhattan—the new home of the Della Femina, McNamee, WCRS advertising agency—fifty-three-year-old Jerry Della Femina strikes an uncharacteristically laid-back pose. The man behind the Fu Manchu mustache is seldom in neutral. Colleagues say he only *visits* his black granite-and-chrome desk, when not rushing to meetings with clients, various industry and civic groups (such as New York's municipal station WNYC-TV, on whose board he serves), or creative review panels. The large poster behind him celebrates the 1987 International Advertising Film Festival at Cannes, where he served as president of the jury.

When he's in the office, he's mostly on the black leather couch (not shown), still doing what he does best—writing copy. The desk—actually more of a group conference table—seems barren, save for some advertising trade journals and a few letters requiring his signature. "It's not that I'm particularly organized but because this place is open to all sorts of traffic—I have an open-door policy—my people make sure there's never anything on it that might fall into the wrong hands." He usually *stands* behind the desk, even when phoning, "because I don't have time to sit."

Besides, he says, he does his best work on his mobile cellular phone. "I may have made medical history the other day when I discovered a new pain syndrome. That is to say, my doctor did. I told him I had this incredible muscular pain in my neck. He knows how much I use the telephone, so he mimicked the way I held the instrument, wedged between chin and shoulder. 'Like this?' he asked. 'Yes,' I said. 'Mmmmmm,' he said, and that was his diagnosis. Cost me a lot of money. I expect to be reading all about it soon in some obscure medical journal."

Now, with feet planted atop the gleaming desktop, Della Femina reminisces. During his messenger days, back in the late 1950s, despairing of ever making more than $37.50 a week, "I used to go into these guys' offices, and most would have their backs to me and their feet up on their desks. One day I asked someone what sort of work these people did. 'Oh, they're in advertising.' 'Wow!' I said. 'That's the business for me. No heavy lifting.'"

No heavy lifting, but a lot of fancy footwork and brilliant (some would use the word "outrageous") advertising campaigns, triggered the opening of his own firm in 1967, after six years of "running it up the flagpole" at five different agencies. Over the next twenty-two years, he parlayed his enterprise into a $600 million multinational megalith, which is still considered one of the "hot creative shops." The various professional awards on his cabinet are one thing; more impressive are such blue-chip clients as American Isuzu Motors, Bausch & Lomb, Chemical Bank, Dow Consumer Brands Inc., Pan American World Airways, Nestlé's, and Beck's beer.

Not shown in this photo is the full-page *New York Times* review of his best-selling book, *From Those Wonderful Folks Who Brought You Pearl Harbor*. The line came out of a stymied Panasonic creative review at the Ted Bates agency, where Della Femina served as creative director for a few months in 1967. What sort of tag line should be used to launch a new Japanese product? "I have it, I have it!" cried the portly, balding young man, whereupon he blurted out the Pearl Harbor line to the shocked executives gathered around the conference table. Soon thereafter, he and art director Ron Travisano left Bates to hang out their own shingle. "I must have been forgiven," he now says. "Joe Isuzu told me so."

Jerry Della Femina continues to make waves. A few years ago, after creating a controversial campaign for prophylactics ("I enjoy sex but I'm not willing to die for it"), he publicly fired the client, who viewed the AIDS crisis as a marketing gold mine.

Della Femina is the father of three grown children from his first marriage and two young ones by his second wife, Fox TV newscaster Judy Licht, whom he met when she interviewed him for a feature on his client the New York Mets. "I'm a born-again father," he exults.

ALAN M. DERSHOWITZ

His operating credo: the means of justice are as important as the ends of justice

Cornered in his Harvard Law School office, bushy-haired Professor Alan M. Dershowitz chomps on a pastrami-on-rye sent over from nearby Maven's—the short-lived kosher deli he and a friend opened (and reluctantly closed) last year after they despaired of waiting for New York's Second Avenue Deli to come to Boston. (The menu reads: "Famous Since 5748," the Hebrew-calendar equivalent to 1988.) He's expounding on the intricate ergometrics of the custom-made teak desk that a Harvard colleague, the architect Ben Thompson, founder of Design Research Inc., had built for him. Many students, observing the shambles he's made of it, have asked if it wouldn't have been cheaper to have gone to the nearest Door Store. "Objection!" cries Dershowitz, pointing out defensively that one man's mess is another's filing system.

Is this the office that launched TV's *The Paper Chase*? "I'm no Professor Kingsfield," insists Dershowitz. "I *thrive* on chaos." He claims that he can tell you where everything is, including his celebrated innumerable spiral-bound notebooks. He neither types nor dictates; everything gets jotted down. As restless as he is voluble, Dershowitz is seldom "at" his desk; instead, he walks around it, talking into his trusty cordless phone, occasionally fishing for a salient document or file.

On the day this picture was shot, there beneath the pastrami sandwich and other detritus lay the manuscript of his latest Random House book, a batch of documents pertaining to the Jonathan Jay Pollard spy case (his current *cause célèbre*), stacks of letters from prisoners all over America who want him to be their "lawyer of last resort," and more of those spiral notebooks.

Pollard, like so many other high-profile clients, came to Dershowitz because of his penchant for taking on cases other lawyers find either undefensible or indefensible. Insisting there is nothing heroic in this line of work, he reaches into his bookshelf to retrieve a Hebrew-lettered plaque bearing an Old Testament line that is Dershowitz's operating credo. "Loosely translated, it says: 'The *means* of justice are as important as the *ends* of justice.'" Clearly, he thinks Pollard—a young U.S. Navy analyst who spied for Israel—got a raw deal. So did an earlier client, Soviet refusenik Natan Shcharansky, whom he defended in a Moscow courtroom more than a decade ago, before his repatriation to Israel (a photograph on Dershowitz's shelf shows Shcharansky nibbling on a Maven's kosher sandwich during a 1988 book promotion tour).

Dershowitz has been winning impossible cases since the mid-1970s, soon after becoming, at age twenty-eight, the youngest fully tenured professor of criminal law in Harvard Law School's 150-year history. He'd served as one of Supreme Court Justice Arthur Goldberg's clerks and, earlier, as a clerk to U.S. Court of Appeals Judge David Bazelon (both of whose framed photos hang on the brick wall, just above those of Dershowitz's other heroes: Golda Meir, retired Boston Celtics coach "Red" Auerbach, and the entire 1955 World Series Brooklyn Dodgers team).

As one of the country's most articulate public defenders of due process, and the only major legal academic with a full-time criminal law practice, Dershowitz knowingly infuriates the legal establishment with such public utterances as: "Beneath the robes of many judges I have seen corruption, incompetence, bias, laziness, meanness of spirit, and plain ordinary stupidity." His outspoken positions have generated a great deal of lunatic-fringe hate mail, some of which he gleefully tapes up outside his door for the enlightenment of his students.

An unabashed nostalgia buff and a consummate collector of such *tchatchkes* as statuettes of Howdy Doody, funny coffee mugs, caricatures, model cars (a pink Caddy commemorates his first used-car purchase as a teenager), and silly gifts presented by his students, Dershowitz also displays multiple copies of his four best-sellers, family photos of his sons, Elon and Jamin, and his second wife, Carolyn, and a Truro, Massachusetts, beach sign outlawing nude bathing—a trophy of one of his sweeter pro bono victories over the forces of bureaucratic mindlessness. In toto, he's created a very unprofessorial study, in which *Blackstone's Commentaries* ranks second to *Dershowitz's Impossible Cases*.

ROGER EBERT

The direction Ebert's thumb takes often determines whether moviegoers go.

An endless flow of cinematic flotsam and jetsam keeps infiltrating the tiny office of the *Chicago Sun-Times*'s Pulitzer Prize–winning film critic, Roger Ebert, and to the despair of the cleaning ladies, none of it appears to be in any hurry to leave. As a result, the janitorial staff now gives his desk wide berth. Like the Water Tower on North Michigan, Ebert's cinematic lair seems to have become a Windy City landmark.

His cherubic countenance is well known to the millions of viewers of *Siskel & Ebert at the Movies*, the weekly TV film-review show on which he appears with—and more often *against*—his co-host and rival, *Chicago Tribune* film critic Gene Siskel. Their show has probably done more to institutionalize the "thumbs up" (or, conversely, "thumbs down") signal for go or no-go than the Indy 500 drivers.

Syndicated nationally, the thirty-minute program is the commercial reincarnation of PBS's *Sneak Previews*, which the two started in 1978.

Celluloid obviously embodies life to Ebert, who joined the paper at age twenty-four, after graduating with a journalism degree from the University of Illinois. "The first movies that really got to me," he recalls, "were animated films like Walt Disney's *Dumbo*. I thought they were real, much more real than photographed movies. And the first movie that made me think I'd make a profession out of moviegoing was *La Dolce Vita*. It broke a lot of rules."

As a critic, so does Ebert, who—pointedly ignoring the late Kenneth Tynan's line: "A critic is like the palace eunuch who sees the trick done every night and rages he can't"—wrote the original screenplay for Russ Meyer's campy *Beyond the Valley of the Dolls* back in 1969.

Those who sometimes find Ebert's preferences too cerebral would be pleasantly surprised to see the critic's likes and dislikes that are flamboyantly displayed in his cluttered cubicle.

An alluring cut-out pinup of Marilyn Monroe in the famous skirt-blowing scene from *The Seven-Year Itch* is propped up in front of Clark Gable and a smoldering Vivien Leigh (*Gone With the Wind*). Original posters from *Casablanca*, *The Wild One*, and *Headline Hunters* are close by.

On Ebert's desk, a gum-ball machine filled with marbles, a Rolodex, and a telephone share equal billing with plastic reproductions of Mickey and Minnie Mouse and Donald Duck. In a jumble of consistent chaos, nearby is a can of Bear B-gone, an "extra strength formula for life's unbearable situations—skunks, raccoons, in-laws, lawyers, bosses"; Metro-Goldwyn-Mayer and Orion Productions paperweights; an "Underworld" miniature typewriter; a three-year-old press pass; and a simulated Venus flytrap from *Little Shop of Horrors*.

On a credenza to the left are copies of Ebert's books, as well as those of his favorite film critics—Pauline Kael, of *The New Yorker*, and Dwight Macdonald, formerly with *Esquire*—and additional mountains of movie compendia. Behind his desk is the ATEX editorial system computer used by writers at the *Sun-Times*.

Sitting serenely in the center of it all is the mainstay of Ebert's professional existence, a portable Tandy Radio Shack Model 100, through which his stories can be sent out via MCI Mail. Ebert takes it everywhere he goes, to facilitate meeting deadlines.

"It's my computer mailbox," he explains. "You can make a local telephone call in Toronto or Cannes and dump it in, and it comes out the other end."

FROM THE DESK OF:

DOUGLAS FAIRBANKS, JR.

Standing at his glass-topped mahogany partners desk, surrounded by a roomful of photographic memorabilia, silver-maned, seventy-nine-year-old Douglas Fairbanks, Jr., refers to himself as the "longest-running Hollywood brat." His father was the famous silent-screen swashbuckler; his stepmother was "America's Sweetheart," Mary Pickford; and his first wife was Joan Crawford ("not the awful person of *Mommie Dearest*"). His wife and close companion of nearly fifty years, interior designer Mary Lee, died in 1988.

The dapper *boulevardier* was the darling of prewar London café society, the fun-loving pal of David Niven, Noel Coward, and Laurence Olivier, the household friend of Admiral Louis Mountbatten and other members of the royal family, and he continues to rekindle our eternal youth as each rerun of *Gunga Din* appears on our home screens. Today the warm, witty, and spectacularly handsome painter, sculptor, sailor, author, and chairman of Fairtel Corporation regales visitors with anecdotes but grows misty when speaking of those who have long since ascended to a higher sound stage.

Fairbanks finds writing infinitely "more satisfying than being a player." He's finishing the second volume of his autobiography (the first, *Salad Days*, came out in 1988). Managing his various transatlantic business ventures also keeps him busy, as does doting on his eight grandchildren, here and abroad.

His midtown New York office, near the Park Avenue apartment he occupies when not in his London or Palm Beach homes, is a Hollywood historian's candy store. Bookcase shelves abound with inscribed portraits and sculpted figures of himself, news photos and candid shots of the great, the near great, and the just plain famous. Framed documents attest to the honorary knighthood he was awarded for organizing Franco-British war relief in 1939 and for other prewar services he performed as the U.S. Navy's liaison to Mountbatten's Commandos, and to his appointment by FDR as special Latin American envoy in 1941; they are interspersed with books by luminaries and cohorts who were his acting peers and with assorted figurines, miniatures, busts, and other works of art.

Then there's the desk, a Victorian beauty, discovered by Mary Lee in a London antique shop. Each picture beneath the glass, every item atop it, carries its own story. Its state of organized disorganization is an act, for on it sits a small leather-bound sign: *Please don't straighten out the Mess on this Desk. You'll Goof Up My System.*

The antique leather desk set, given to him by his dear friend the producer David O. Selznick, reminds him of the revelry and rivalry that took place on the set of *The Prisoner of Zenda*, one of the seventy-odd movies he made in the thirties and forties. A photo of Fairbanks's bust of Marlene Dietrich on his desktop and a figurine of Greta Garbo peering out from a low shelf evoke warm memories, as does the deck of Players cigarette cards bearing the profiles of Fairbanks *père et fils*. "I had no particular desire to be a carbon-copy personality of my father, nor was I equipped to be one. I was determined to be my own man, although having the Fairbanks name sometimes made it easier to get in to see someone at the studio," he says. At the same time, he adds, "It led people to expect too much from an inexperienced, undereducated boy—and I was apt to be fired that much earlier!"

DEBBI FIELDS

With oat bran on
everyone's lips,
Mrs. Fields now
offers oat
cuisine,
too.

Yes, there actually *is* a Mrs. Fields, as in Mrs. Fields Cookies, and she's not a gray-haired granny from Grinnell, nor someone sent over from central casting to play a living corporate symbol à la Betty Crocker. Seen here in her combination executive suite and private day-care center in Park City, Utah, is Debra Jane Fields, a stunning thirty-one-year-old blue-eyed blonde from Oakland, California.

Starting in 1977 with a $50,000 loan from her financial-consultant husband, Randall (now forty-one and Mrs. Fields's board chairman), charismatic Debbi Fields parlayed a Palo Alto ministore into a $170-million multinational—the world's largest family-owned chain of specialty food shops.

Along the way, she also found time to raise four daughters, the youngest of whom, one-and-a-half-year-old Ashley, is seen here occupying her own toy-strewn area next to her mother's Renaissance Revival oak desk, bought in 1980 at auction in nearby Salt Lake City for $300.

Whereas most women executives will try to downplay their distaff roles by keeping just one, perhaps two, framed photographs of husband and children in view, Fields proudly displays all sorts of family photos, valentine-framed drawings, love poems, schoolwork by her daughters, and other "sentimental things," which make this basement office seem less a powerhouse than a playroom. In the bookcase behind her is part of a Cookie Bear uniform that staff volunteers sometimes slip into before visiting children in nearby hospitals, armed with tins of cookies and brownies.

There's also an inexplicable set of motorized false teeth someone gave her "because people think I talk too fast."

Motivation is her forte and the company's secret weapon in the very competitive war with hordes of come-and-go imitators. She's the first to bear good tidings, usually by sounding a New Year's Eve horn or noisemaker she keeps conveniently in her desk drawer.

Constantly on the go, spending two or three days each week away from her desk, Fields feels the need to get in as much quality time with her children as possible. Last year she logged over 350,000 air miles visiting stores in the U.S. and overseas (where she often manned the counters herself), speaking before trade groups, and making guest TV appearances. So hectic is her schedule that Debbi Fields (who does everything by the book, in this case the Franklin Day Planner next to the phone) has learned to do things by countdown calendar; "22 days until bran muffin intro . . ."

She plays the telephone like a virtuoso, calling store managers, dispensing goodwill, sage advice, and reminders that the company's credo ("Good Enough Never Is") isn't just a clever advertising slogan.

On the days she's in, it's open house. With the people upstairs in the Willie Wonka–type chocolate factory sending down new goodies for "executive review," the staff finds excuses to traipse in and out of her office. "It's like the best place to eat in Park City is 'Debbi's Place,' " sighs Debbi, pushing a round candy dish filled with chocolate chips at the visitor. "I always have tons of candy on hand."

Yet, while admitting to being a junk food junkie, she won't keep any cookies on her desk. Too tempting, apparently. The CEO's R and D lot is not an easy one: she has to go through at least ten tastings a day. But her energy-burning trips help balance the scales: she has told reporters she now weighs twenty pounds *less* than the day she started the business.

A little-known fact that you won't find in the almanac is that Utah has the highest per capita chocolate consumption of any of the fifty states. Another fact: Utah has the world's second-highest birth rate after Bangladesh. Make of these two facts what you will.

FRANK GEHRY

Gehry's Walt Disney Concert Hall design bested heavy international competition.

L.A. MUSIC CENTER

Seated in one of his award-winning corrugated-cardboard easy chairs, next to his custom-designed tool- and toy-strewn plywood desk/credenza (which he seldom uses, as he prefers working next door with his design team), Canadian-born, California-based architect Frank Gehry is feeling particularly comfortable. It's not the chair but the satisfaction of having just won the global competition for the plum of plums: the commission for the new $100 million home of the Los Angeles Philharmonic.

Last winter, to the astonishment (and envy) of the nation's architectural establishment, the twenty-seven-year-old firm of Frank O. Gehry & Associates of Santa Monica—until then known mainly for its principal's playfully contradictory "deconstructionist" style of deploying tilted beams, warped walls, unsettling angles—triumphed over three of Europe's most prestigious architects for a 2,500-seat concert hall and 1,000-seat chamber music annex to rise next to the Dorothy Chandler Pavilion in the Los Angeles Music Center Complex.

Come 1993, when the orchestra moves into the new home that will replace the outmoded twenty-five-year-old Chandler Pavilion—site of the annual Academy Awards ceremony—Gehry's Walt Disney Concert Hall will almost certainly shatter the pristine but boring orderliness of that downtown quadrangle. Much as this prospect pleases the trustees of the Disney estate (who are putting up half the money), their delight can't come close to that of sixty-year-old Gehry, whose history of rule-breaking gives new meaning to the word "controversial." In Los Angeles, he's built private homes (including his own) that have been de-scribed as "explosions in a chopstick factory"—an allusion to his unconventional use of such harsh materials as unfinished timber, chain-link fencing, and metal sheeting. With Claes Oldenburg, he's designed a campy camp for terminally ill children under the auspices of the McDonald Corporation. Again with the avant-garde sculptor, Gehry recently finished a building for which Oldenburg designed a frontage resembling a pair of binoculars—hence the binoculars on the desk, a gift from the artist, who also gave him the white "Swiss Army Knife" kinetic sculpture to the left of them. In Kobe, Japan, Gehry has built a restaurant that resembles a giant carp (his obsession with fish shapes shows up in much of his work and throughout this office). Partnered with adman Jay Chiat (whose agency has a fish-shaped dining room), he's building *San'wiches*, a chain of robot-manned fast-food restaurants Gehry describes as "mini contemporary art museums that happen to serve great food."

An editor at *Architectural Record* dismisses Gehry's work as "transitionally quintessential Southern Californian," but the rules Gehry breaks today will undoubtedly be tomorrow's orthodoxy. It's an unfair characterization that ignores such out-of-state work as Gehry's trend-setting "new town" civic architecture at Columbia, Maryland; the mid-Atlantic corporate headquarters of Toyota; the Laser Laboratories at the University of Iowa (model seen here through the window); and a planned New York City highrise (model on top of the desk). Back home, between visiting professorships at Harvard, Yale, and UCLA, Gehry has designed Loyola University's Law School and the famed jazz music pavilion in Concord, re-engineered the acoustics of the Hollywood Bowl, and created an exposition center and shopping mall in Santa Monica "for people who hate malls" (to quote one rave review).

But until Gehry won that competition for Disney Hall, says the critic Joseph Morgenstern, "he was that iconoclast you kept reading intriguing articles about, the guy invited to chic dinner parties, even hired to build audacious houses, but not one you gave major public commissions to."

That was then. This is now.

STEPHEN JAY GOULD

Newsweek,
3/29/82,
graphic by
Ib Ohlsson

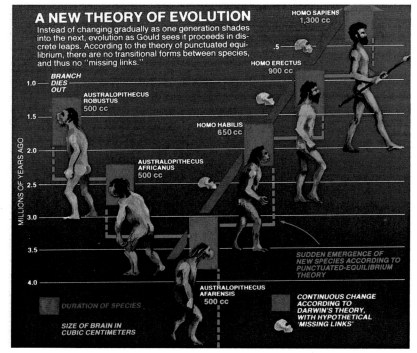

A NEW THEORY OF EVOLUTION
Instead of changing gradually as one generation shades into the next, evolution as Gould sees it proceeds in discrete leaps. According to the theory of punctuated equilibrium, there are no transitional forms between species, and thus no "missing links."

HOMO SAPIENS
1,300 cc

HOMO ERECTUS
900 cc

BRANCH
DIES
OUT

AUSTRALOPITHECUS
ROBUSTUS
500 cc

HOMO HABILIS
650 cc

AUSTRALOPITHECUS
AFRICANUS
500 cc

MILLIONS OF YEARS AGO

SUDDEN EMERGENCE OF
NEW SPECIES ACCORDING TO
PUNCTUATED-EQUILIBRIUM
THEORY

AUSTRALOPITHECUS
AFARENSIS
500 cc

CONTINUOUS CHANGE
ACCORDING TO
DARWIN'S THEORY,
WITH HYPOTHETICAL
'MISSING LINKS'

DURATION OF SPECIES

SIZE OF BRAIN IN
CUBIC CENTIMETERS

When America's foremost writer and thinker on evolution, Dr. Stephen Jay Gould, forty-seven, isn't on one of his many field trips to the Bahamas, where he hunts down land snails of the genus *Cerion,* or teaching biology, geology, or the history of science, or on the road with his anticreationism lectures, he can be found at one of the two desks he uses in a cramped corner of a cavernous hall in Harvard's MCZ (Museum of Comparative Zoology).

The desk shown contains the slides and fossils basic to Gould's work as an evolutionary biologist on Harvard's faculty, with titles of Professor of Geology and Curator of Invertebrate Paleontology. The second desk, fifteen feet away, holds his phone, daily mail, microscope, and memos, as well as research studies relating to his twenty-two years of teaching at Cam-

bridge. Gould is as prolific as he is astute, and his sixteen years of monthly columns in *Natural History* magazine and frequent articles in *Discover* have evolved into such renowned books as *The Panda's Thumb, The Flamingo's Smile, Ever Since Darwin,* and *The Mismeasure of Man,* which won the 1981 National Book Critics Circle Award.

He says he's "not afraid to try and write about baseball, choral music, and dinosaurs in the same week and see connections among them." But Gould doesn't write at either of his two office desks. He prefers to write in his Cambridge home, where the environment is more

congenial to his eclectic muse.

His work space in the 130-year-old museum building has aspects of an archaeological dig. While preparing to repaint the place a few years ago, workers discovered writing on the wall. Gould had them scrub away the surface soil to reveal the nineteenth-century exhibit titles from the room's heyday: *Synopsis of the Animal Kingdom* and such inscriptions as *Vertebrates: Class of Amphibians.*

The fourteen-foot-high wall is lined with a reef of fossil cases, and shelf labels read *Southampton, Eastern Bermuda,* and other locales where Gould garners his land snails. Over the years, he's

reclassified a once-perceived genus of six hundred species to a more legitimate count of fewer than twenty. A more significant contribution to his field is the new theory of evolution he propounded in 1972 with collaborator Niles Eldredge, paleontologist with the American Museum of Natural History: "punctuated equilibrium." Their theory holds that evolution proceeds in leaps rather than in gradual shades.

Gould is one of the leading critics of "creationism," the fundamentalist explanation of the world's genesis, and he speaks often, far and wide, as a highly effective defender of evolutionary enlightenment. That professional zeal spills over to his hacker's love of baseball, with the diamond-clear evidence displayed around his desks—a caricature of a uniformed Gould pitching, a stuffed dinosaur doll wearing a baseball cap, and a photo of himself and his son with Joe DiMaggio.

While everything is up-to-date in Gould's thinking, his material trappings indicate an affinity for the old, the tried, and the true. The easy chair next to his desk is bursting through its threadbare covering, the worn bazaar carpet purchased in Istanbul is near a well-deserved extinction, and his battered briefcase, replete with Bahamian travel stickers, looks as though it may have taken its last trip. In Gould's world, things don't have to be the fittest to survive.

CATHY GUISEWITE

cathy® 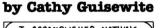 **by Cathy Guisewite**

"I go through a lot of M & M's," confesses Cathy Guisewite, the thirty-eight-year-old West Coast cartoonist/chronicler of the foibles and follies of the working single woman who just happens to bear her creator's name. Since the daily comic strip *Cathy*, syndicated to over five hundred newspapers coast to coast, is obviously based on the cartoonist's own life encounters, it should come as no surprise that both continue to search for a diet that calls for a daily fix of candy-coated chocolate pills.

It's just one of the ways that Ms. Guisewite uses her strip as a forum from which to tackle certain social issues common to millions of her loyal readers.

Guisewite relies mainly on three central characters: Cathy, her mother, and Andrea, the opinionated best friend, who sounds off on women's issues, politics, and morality. A new strip character, Electra, is modeled after Trolley, Guisewite's collie-shepherd.

Tucked away in a sprawling ranch house near Laurel Canyon in Los Angeles, Guisewite's studio is an unlikely mixture of high-tech efficiency and California mellow. Within arm's reach of a layout pad, India ink, and white-out bottles, the cartoonist is off and running at her drawing table by 8:45 each morning, working left-handed on "whatever is most hideously overdue."

Her projects range from turning out her wildly popular daily strip and monthly *Glamour* magazine piece, to conceiving *Cathy* calendars, mugs, Post-it notes, and greeting cards, as well as books and TV storyboards for a series of animated *Cathy* specials for CBS, the first of which received an Emmy. Cathy's lovable ups and downs in the turbulent sea of singledom have earned her creator over seventy million readers and a hefty six-figure income.

Guisewite's comfortable wooden two-drawer desk is equipped with an old eight ball that magically answers "yes," "no," or "maybe" to whatever questions its possessor asks of it. "Although it hasn't been instrumental in my decision making," she says, "it's good to get a second opinion." There is also a Hyundai computer; a Cathy mug that proclaims: "My love for you is a bottomless pit"; the omnipresent jar of M & M's; and a copy of Guisewite's real mom's new book, *Motherly Advice from Cathy's Mother*.

Except for a black-and-white photograph of the cartoonist accepting her Emmy, there are no awards, personal photographs, or drawings of her own anywhere in sight. Instead there is a vase of flowers, a drawing of her by her young niece, a stained-glass Cathy made by a friend, and a file cabinet heaped with papers. On the floor is a life-size Cathy doll and, on most days, the canine Trolley snoozing beneath the desk.

With its sweeping view of the Santa Monica mountains, Guisewite's studio is a far cry from the Detroit advertising agency where she worked as a copywriter before launching *Cathy* in 1976. *Cathy* began in some ways like Beatrix Potter's *Peter Rabbit*. Guisewite sent her mother illustrated letters that highlighted the humorous side of her workdays. "Mom persuaded me to send samples of the drawings to Universal Press Syndicate, and to my amazement, I got a contract back in the mail shortly afterward. As difficult as it may seem to people who can't separate the idealized version of Cathy from the genuine article, I always know in my mind that line where her life ends and mine begins."

AL HIRSCHFELD

**Hirschfeld does
Hirschfeld.**

In the sun-flooded fourth-floor studio of his red-brick Victorian townhouse in Manhattan, surrounded by legions of his Broadway "friends," Al Hirschfeld leans back in his barber chair, looks up from that day's portrait (of B. D. Wong in *M. Butterfly*), and ruminates. "It is never my aim to destroy the play or the performer with ridicule. I want to take the character as created by the playwright and acted out by the actor and to reinvent it for the reader."

At age eighty-six, the patriarchal Hirschfeld, who started out as a seventeen-year-old art director for Samuel Goldwyn in the days of the silent screen, is still bestowing instant fame on those the *New York Times* sees fit to showcase in its Sunday and Friday drama pages. (As veteran drama critic Brendan Gill put it, there are two ways of defining fame on Broadway: to see your name in lights and, "more signif-

icantly, to be drawn by Hirschfeld.") Over the past sixty-plus years, seated in slippers in an antique "Koken" barber chair he picked up for ten dollars on the Bowery and poised above a deeply scarred wooden drawing table, the hirsute Hirschfeld has created more than three thousand pen-and-ink drawings of ensembles and individuals—most of them instantly recognizable to the cognoscenti and thus in no need of identifying labels.

While Hirschfeld is most closely associated with the *New York Times*, his art has been commissioned by other newspapers, by book and magazine publishers, by TV networks, and by the U.S. Postal Service, for which he designed a series of twenty-five-cent stamps honoring great performers and entertainers. All of his original artwork is sold through the Margo Feiden Galleries in New York.

Hirschfeld seems incapable of inflicting malice—for most "caricaturists," a professional hazard. Years ago, art historian Lloyd Goodrich, in the introduction to a Hirschfeld anthology, wrote that the artist "is affirmative, friendly, good-hearted and honest; qualities that—while not harmful to a saint—might prove great handicaps to one whose success depends on his calling the world's attention to the physical oddities of others."

Hirschfeld in fact bridles at being called a caricaturist, insisting that caricature is usually seen as "negative," because the artist—by focusing on physiognomy—maliciously distorts the truth, turning subject into victim. Not Hirschfeld, who always accentuates the positive, even if personally he believes the play is doomed. "No one is more eager than he that the theater be seen at its best," says Brendan Gill. "Whatever the show's eventual fate, Al will have given it a rousing send-off."

Hirschfeld admits he loves the theater and theater people, especially people like Carol Channing or the late Zero Mostel—"the explosive actors, the glandular actors, the ones with bulging eyes who don't close doors but *slam* them." He married an actress (Dolly Haas, the mother of Nina, who, now forty-four and herself a parent, has been a nominal presence in

her father's drawings from childhood), and he calls himself a "failed playwright"—a reference to the 1946 musical he collaborated on with Ogden Nash, S. J. Perelman, and Vernon Duke, *Sweet Bye and Bye*, which starred Dolores Grey and flopped in Philadelphia.

Hirschfeld has sat in the dark through many hundreds of rehearsals and out-of-town tryouts, rough-sketching the actors on stage and furiously scribbling descriptive notes that only he can decipher when the lights come up. "Mine is a collaboration of sight and hand, with no conscious thought at the controls." After the curtain falls, he rushes backstage to catch the actors in costume for a fast "academic eye-ear-nose-and-throat" sketch. "Visual memory is tricky and not always reliable," he admits. Then, back at his studio, he parks himself before a 20-by-30-inch piece of triple-ply, cold-pressed illustration board, and using a Guillot quill pen dipped in India ink, turns his penciled sketches and notes into a large drawing. Hirschfeld no longer works to "specs" other than his own. "The size of my drawing is determined only by the demands of the drawing. I have long ago given up the losing battle of layouts."

GEOFFREY HOLDER

A giant talent, Holder is equally at home at the typewriter, camera, easel, or on stage.

One reason why there is no desk, in the conventional sense, to be found anywhere in the cavernous SoHo loft that is both home and office to quintuple-threat artist/showman Geoffrey Holder and his dancer wife Carmen De Lavallade (partially seen in the painting directly behind Holder) is that he's into so many different things at once that so static a piece of furniture would only impede the flow of his creative juices. "I do my best work as I roam. A desk would force me to focus on trivial details. Besides," he adds in his familiar, mellifluous *basso profundo*, "now that God in His infinite wisdom has given us the portable telephone, I'm no longer dependent on being tethered to a wall jack."

The juices don't just flow, they *cascade*. There are few things the tall (six-foot-four-inch) Trinidad-born Holder hasn't tried—and triumphantly,

exuberantly so. He first drew public acclaim as the principal dancer in the 1954 Harold Arlen–Truman Capote Broadway musical, *House of Flowers*, starring Pearl Bailey, Juanita Hall, and Diahann Carroll. (During the run of the show he met De Lavallade, whom he married six months later.)

While in ballet, he was also seen as premier danseur in such Metropolitan Opera productions as *Aïda* and *La Périchole*. One of his memorable dramatic roles was as Lucky in a 1957 production of Beckett's *Waiting for Godot*.

Filmgoers who may have forgotten his cameo appearance in the Woody Allen film *Everything You Always Wanted to Know About Sex* (1972) will surely remember him as the evil Baron Samedi in the first Roger Moore/James Bond film, *Live and Let Die* (which he also choreographed), and as Daddy Warbucks' faithful Punjab in the 1982 movie version of *Annie*.

On television, his Cheshire Cat opposite Richard Burton and daughter Kate in *Alice in Wonderland*, and his performance vis-à-vis Noel Coward in George Bernard Shaw's *Androcles and the Lion* were enthusiastically received, but they pale in memory next to his Clio-winning commercials for 7-Up soda and British West Indian Airlines.

Still, he is most honored for his nonacting backstage roles,

mainly as the Tony Award–winning director and costume designer for *The Wiz* in the 1974–75 season and for directing, choreographing, and costuming *Timbuktu!* with Eartha Kitt in 1977–78. Though retired as a dancer, he is indispensable to the world-renowned Dance Theatre of Harlem, which he serves as choreographer as well as costume and set designer.

As if this weren't enough, there's his professional photography (collected in a Viking publication a few years ago) and his writing—a cookbook and the nonfiction volume *Black Gods, Green Islands*.

He also does a lot of painting, for which he won a Guggenheim grant. Holder's oils are much sought after and are in a number of permanent museum collections, including the Corcoran Gallery, the Barbados Museum, and the Museum of the City of New York. He even painted the thirty-foot mural in the Trinidad Hilton.

"My desk is wherever I happen to be at a given moment. Right now, my desk is an easel," says Holder.

New York City, he insists, "is the only city I can live in, if only for its taxis. I don't drive a car. Since I paint, I need to get my art over to the galleries. As a result, I *live* in taxis. You might say they're my *rolling* desk."

FROM THE DESK OF:

BETSEY JOHNSON

The funky, free-spirited Johnson hangs out on her lively fashions across the U.S.A.

"Some of the out-of-town buyers who come here for the first time do look a little dazed," admits Betsey Johnson, grinning broadly. "But they all love to come back."

There's no mistaking the identity of the tenant on this floor. Johnson's signature hot-pink neon sign really is her signature, and it matches the signs at all her boutiques, for which she personally hand-paints the murals.

"Isn't it fabulous?" exclaims Johnson, as she whirls through her showroom/workroom/offices, located in New York's garment district, one flight up from Lou G. Siegel's kosher restaurant. She eyes a half-dozen new bolts of shimmering latex fabric that will soon turn into frothy, slinky, zany outfits that spell s-e-x a-p-p-e-a-l. Rock music suffuses the air, high-speed assistants whiz through the offices, and phones ring constantly.

The effervescent designer maintains the average daily momentum of a cyclone in overseeing her eight U.S. boutiques (three in New York and one each in Boston, Los Angeles, San Francisco, Venice, and Coconut Grove), the manufacturing of labels, and the invention of her refreshingly unconventional clothes, which are usually designed two seasons in advance. These outrageous outfits combine Johnson's zest for fifties cheerleading, sixties hippie styles, and seventies body-hugging fashions.

On this particular day, she sports a belt with wildly dyed rabbit's feet swaying to and fro, a full skirt, leotarded legs, a junk-store heart-shaped medallion, and hair that could easily be mistaken for a punked-out rainbow in Tibet.

The large plywood cutting table that serves as her desk is easily twenty feet long. Located at the far end of a vast workroom, it is generously heaped with fascinating fragments of the designer's day-to-day creative life. Explosively colored silk flowers are wedged in between baskets of swatches, bolts of fabric, multicolored pens and markers, a pair of ten-inch cutting shears, and an eight-button phone with a mile-long cord.

Articles of clothing, design drawings, costume jewelry, hats, and a thousand other items fall from the board to the floor, near a tiny child mannequin decorated with beads of Johnson's design.

There is an institutional-sized jar of Orville Redenbacher's Popping Corn (the popper is within arm's reach), a shelf of work files, folios with designs for Johnson's upcoming line, and a large black-and-white photograph of her fifteen-year-old daughter, Lulu. ("My clothes aren't sophisticated enough for her," says her mother.)

Every time Johnson plans a new collection, she and Lulu escape city life and head to their country home in upstate New York, where they tool around in a yellow Mercedes-Benz convertible ("it *should* be a pickup truck") and visit the local ShopRite ("where I get some of my best ideas").

On the bulletin board to the right of her desk is a note from her Doubleday editor: "Looking forward to the publication of your book!"

"I'm collaborating with a writer on my biography," says Johnson, who plans on opening two additional boutiques a year for the next five years. "I wonder if I'll ever have time to read it."

JACKIE JOYNER-KERSEE

Everybody's *Athlete of the Year*, and an Olympian role model to kids.

At her desk in the converted garage that serves as her office in Long Beach, California, long-legged and fleet-footed Jacqueline Joyner-Kersee seems to find momentary respite from the media mania that dogs her every appearance. But not for long.

Having won virtually every race she's ever entered, Jackie Joyner-Kersee—whose Seoul-ful performance during the 1988 Summer Olympics in South Korea prompted macho *Sporting News* to name her Athlete of the Year (the first woman so named in the publication's twenty-year history)—has discovered that the more prizes she wins, the harder it gets to streak by the reporters.

Now that her charismatic gold-medal-winning sister-in-law, Florence Griffith-Joyner ("Flo-Jo"), has hung up her Adidas for good to pursue an acting career, Jackie had better get used to even more of the attention that's landed her on the covers of *Time*, and *Sports Illustrated*.

But there is another, lesser-known role Jackie Joyner-Kersee plays off-track, one the sports press seldom covers: that of role model to tens of thousands of inner-city kids. It's clearly an exhilarating new game for the twenty-seven-year-old sprinter from economically devastated East Saint Louis, Illinois—just across the Mississippi and light-years away from the 7-Up Company, whose soft drink she endorses and whose royalties she pours into the JJK Foundation, which she set up last year.

Its slogan—"Be What You Want to Be"—and its "3-D Philosophy" (Desire, Dedication, Determination) sum up JJK's *modus vivendi*. At every opportunity, she drops in on local black ghetto community centers like the ones in which she hung out growing up in southern Illinois. There she pep-talks her young fans into shaping up, intellectually as well as physically. Drawing audiences is the easiest part, say community activists. "She's the honey for the bees."

As a beehive, the office is perfectly color-coordinated, and the dark, wood-grained cabinets and matching desk stand out nicely against the beige walls and light carpeting. The room could easily pass as one woman's Hall of Fame, given the number of medallions, cups, statuettes, and plaques on exhibit or hung from the walls. Each trophy has its own story: the USOC-AAU James E. Sullivan Award naming her the nation's top all-around amateur athlete for 1987; the Dunlop Award for 1986; the Broderick Cup for outstanding 1984–85 Collegiate Woman Athlete; and the recent Grand Prix for indoor field and track.

On the wall hangs a plaque that honors Jackie's induction into the nearby San Pedro Sportswalk—the athlete's version of Hollywood Boulevard's "Walk of Stars," only harder to get into.

One item of prominence on the desk that seems very much out of place is the large bag of potato chips. Is this the breakfast of champions? "Believe it or not, it used to be for me, but that was long ago, when I was a kid. I used to eat 'em for breakfast, for lunch, for dinner—all the time."

Her husband and coach, Bob Kersee, shoots her a disapproving glance. She catches it. "Right now it's OK to eat them, 'cause I'm not in training. Truth is," she whispers, "I'm really into junk food." Incidentally, her favorite beverage is not Gatorade but the "Un-cola," which—her sponsor will be overjoyed to hear—she drinks "by the case." Unsurprisingly, an exercycle stands to the right of the desk.

For all the accolades showered upon her, Jackie Joyner-Kersee has definitely not "gone Hollywood." This becomes evident as she picks up the letter opener on the desk—a promotional gift from the friendly folks at Security Pacific Bank; it has a quarter, a dime, and a nickel embedded in the Lucite shaft. "You know what this means?" she asks. "It means I've got forty cents to my name." Not quite.

FROM THE DESK OF:

SENATOR NANCY L. KASSEBAUM

The senator is very much at home at her home away from home.

"Toto, I've a feeling we're not in Kansas anymore."

During her 1979 maiden speech to the National Press Club, Republican Senator Nancy Landon Kassebaum of Kansas instantly won over Washington's cynical press corps when she departed from her text and said, "Toto, I've a feeling we're not in Kansas anymore."

Indeed she wasn't. But as the daughter of 1936 GOP presidential candidate Alfred M. Landon and a person literally weaned on politics—she spent the first four years of her life in the Kansas governor's mansion—Senator Kassebaum makes sure that when she's in her plant-strewn chambers in the Russell Senate Office Building, she'll never be far from home. RSOB Suite 302 is awash with so many Sunflower State artifacts that her staff now places important telephone messages on her leather swivel chair, lest

they go unseen amid the assorted clutter on her Bunyanesque desk—a hand-me-down from the suite's previous occupant, former Minnesota Senator Wendell Anderson.

Unlike some of her sister legislators over in the House, Senator Kassebaum never sought to redecorate her working quarters but held on to the heavy mahogany furniture designed for occupants much larger than she. It doesn't upset her in the least. At age fifty-seven, divorced in 1979 after twenty-four years of marriage (to Kansas broadcast executive J. Philip Kassebaum) and the mother of four grown-ups, she's not about to become a militant feminist.

Whether out of political design (for impressing visiting constituents), or her well-known passion for collecting memorabilia, the accumulation on her desk leaves no doubt as to

where Nancy Kassebaum stands—or, as the case may be, *sits*. A conservative with centrist leanings, the senator is first and foremost a Kansas booster.

More than half the glass-topped surface of the desk is taken up by such obviously sentimental made-in-Kansas or by-Kansans doodads as: a carved wooden buffalo (a gift from the Ness County Farm Bureau); a sculpted University of Kansas Jayhawk; a cast-iron elephant coin bank (one of dozens of GOP pachyderms that ended up in her office); a milkweed-embedded crystal paperweight; notepads imprinted with the famous Toto line; and the inevitable baseball cap, found in virtually every senatorial office—this one from the 1985 World Champion Kansas City Royals.

On the credenza by the window, next to a gray flannel stuffed elephant and a group photo of Ronald and Nancy Reagan paying a hundredth-birthday visit to the patriarch Alf Landon, Senator Kassebaum keeps an autographed basketball given her by the 1988 University of Kansas national championship basketball team. There are books about Kansas by Kan-

sans on the window ledge and on every table. The glass-paneled bookcase by her desk is chockablock with representations of Kansas sunflowers, sculptures made of Kansas wheat, and awards from various groups and associations. On one wall hangs a series of Kansas landscape scenes by a noted state artist. In the reception room, a huge green-and-white patchwork quilt depicts highlights of Nancy Landon Kassebaum's life. Fabricated by current and former members of her staff, the quilt was presented to her on her fifty-fifth birthday.

There are only a few exceptions to the Kansas theme: a ceramic elephant from India, which serves as the senator's desktop rubber band dispenser; a miniature locomotive atop a trestle on the senator's desk; and a Zulu tribal cane leaning against the credenza. These are gifts related to her work on various Senate committees.

Toto understands . . .

LARRY KING

Once Larry Zeigler of Brooklyn, now he's Larry King of the airwaves, interviewing a thousand greats, near-greats, and ingrates each year for fun and profit.

It is Wednesday afternoon in Arlington, Virginia, and Larry King, America's best-known conversationalist, is at home—wrestling with another medium. Dressed in his working (not walking) shorts, sitting in a cane-backed dining chair draped with the harness racer's jacket he will wear for George Plimpton's celebrity trot, in which he intends to drive a sulky, King pulls up to the desk given him five years ago by his daughter Chaia, now a Goucher College senior. He negotiates the Smith-Corona as easily as if it were an open mike. "I took typing lessons at P.S. 128, Brooklyn."

He's under the gun because the people up the street at *USA Today* have just called to ask when they may expect his weekly column, "Larry King's People." He's not sure.

King is used to deadlines, whether on the 350-plus syndicated radio stations that carry *The Larry King Show* (Monday–Friday, 11:00 P.M.–2:00 A.M. EST) or on CNN's *Larry King Live* (Monday–Friday, 9:00 P.M.–10:00 P.M. EST).

It's a grind that would easily tax anyone, let alone a fifty-six-year-old who two years ago underwent a quintuple-bypass operation and who now says, "The greatest thing that ever happened to me was waking up after the operation—and winning the [George Foster] Peabody Award," radio's equivalent of the Oscar. He is also a three-time winner of the Ace Award for "top cable personality."

Over the chair nearest his bookcase and fronting his modern mahogany desk are his "civilian duds"—the clothes he'll slip into fast when the limousine comes to whisk him across the Potomac to the CNN studios in downtown Washington.

The chair to the right sports a monogrammed Baltimore Orioles baseball jacket. The former Larry Zeigler, the Russian immigrants' kid who grew up in the shadow of Brooklyn's Ebbets Field, is now an Orioles booster.

Neatly arranged on the desk's "balcony" are items from Super Bowl XX, the '86 All-Stars game in Houston, and, flanking a Sony Watchman, other championship games.

King relishes the pace and loves his work. "Just think, five nights a week I get to meet the most interesting people in the world and ask them *anything* I want, and I get paid for it." *Well* paid, too. CNN pays him $800,000, Mutual $400,000, and Gannett doesn't stint, nor do those who clamor to have him address their conventions and fund-raisers. He takes a sanguine view of celebrity: "I'm told Phil Donahue makes almost three times as much for working a fraction of the hours I do. *Big* deal. Phil can buy a ninety-six-foot yacht, while I can only buy a forty-eight-foot yacht."

He's been on the air thirty-two years—first as a pinch-hit announcer on a 25-watt Florida radio station, then as host of a man-off-the-street interview show emanating from a Miami Beach restaurant, moving up to the networks before experiencing a humiliating fall from grace when his profligate ways landed him in bankruptcy court. King figures he's interviewed more than thirty thousand people; the *Guinness Book of World Records* commends him for having logged more airtime than anyone in his field.

He's been interviewing people since he was an eight-year-old. "I used to ask, 'Why do you drive a bus?' or 'What's good about being a cop?'" These days, the people he confronts come from headier stock. His favorites are former Senator Barry Goldwater ("blunt but endearing"), New York Governor Mario Cuomo ("the best 'listen' of all"), Dudley Moore ("I can recite his 'One-Legged Tarzan' number by heart"), and Frank Sinatra ("very complex").

Last Christmas, Sinatra sent him a case of wine; it reposes next to the Louisville Slugger leaning against the bookcase. "Would you believe it, he thanked *me* for having him on the program!" Equally welcome was the oversize get-well card from Mickey Mouse's employer, Disney Studio head Michael Eisner, which King intends to have framed.

As to all those books sent by publishers: "I make it a point not to read them before meeting their authors. I won't prepare my questions, because that would make the answers—well—*predictable.*" One for whom he would have made an exception was Cole Porter. "I'm into lyricists," King says, and he reaches for *The Complete Works of Cole Porter* on his desk.

"Boy, would I have had questions to ask *him!*"

FROM THE DESK OF:

MAYOR ED KOCH

The first NYC mayor to use Koch's desk was the legendary "Little Flower," Fiorello H. La Guardia.

THE MUSEUM OF THE CITY OF NEW YORK

"I never sit, I *stand*," insists that consummate New Yorker, tall and feisty Edward Irving Koch, who appears to be in perpetual motion even when he does stand. At a very spry sixty-five, the nation's best-known, most visual and outrageously vocal municipal chief executive clearly loves his job—which he's held since 1978—enough to try for four more years.

Each weekday morning, after a workout in the gym, Koch arrives promptly at seven-thirty in his suite at the northwest corner of historic (1811) City Hall, having—on the drive down from Gracie Mansion—already zipped through four New York dailies. He spends the first hour giving dictation, not at his desk but off camera, in an easy chair. The only time he actually works at the ornate glass-topped Federal-style desk—which serves mainly as a place to keep

papers and as a showcase for souvenirs from his trips abroad and gifts from foreign visitors—is to sign his correspondence or any proclamations sent over by his Special Events office. The desk, he explains, is "too low to comfortably sit at, and too high when raised on special blocks."

The desk was "inherited" from New York's legendary, equally flamboyant mayor, Fiorello H. La Guardia (1934–45). Koch discovered it in dilapidated condition in the corridor outside his office, transplanted the "temp" using it that day, and had it refurbished. Its most significant artifact is the old WNYC microphone the "Little Flower" used when he read the "funnies" to New York's comics-starved children during the 1945 newspaper strike. Dearer to Koch are sundry souvenirs picked up in the course of his globe-trotting—a malachite incense burner, Foo dogs, and a Buddha from China; various tiny camels from the Near East; an Easter Island statuette; a snuffbox from France; and, inevitably, more than one Steuben crystal apple. In between are various awards that were showered upon him by such grateful constituents as the Screen Directors Guild, the New School for Social Research, and the American Academy of Professional Law

Enforcement. At the front of the desk is a mounted biblical quotation a friend sent the mayor following his 1987 stroke (from which he completely recovered):

If you pass through raging waters in the sea, you shall not drown. If you walk 'mid the burning flames, you shall not be harmed. If you stand before the power of hell, and death is at your side, know that I am with you through it all.

(Since this photo was taken, the sign has been replaced by one with the mayor's favorite slogan: "The Truth Is Still Relevant.")

On the credenza behind Koch is a multibutton phone he seldom uses (preferring the one by the easy chair) and stacks of books the mayor is reading or wishes he had time to read—diet books, novels, and New York City history books, sent him by various publishers. The framed oil behind Koch—a 1910 Paris street scene by Childe Hassam—is one of a rotating series of paintings on loan from the Metropolitan Museum of Art, which the mayor frequently strolls through—as a paying visitor.

JULIE KRONE

The winningest woman in the history of racing, Krone does it again.

WIDE WORLD

Just twenty furlongs from Belmont Race Track, Julie Krone, the world's winningest woman jockey, whip in hand, bestrides the desk at her home in Elmont, Long Island, demonstrating her phenomenally successful racing form.

The twenty-six-year-old Krone, first jockey ever to win six races in one day (Monmouth, '87), is currently the leading jockey of either sex at nearby Aqueduct. At the track, she is known among her "Kronies" as a no-nonsense competitor. At home, her madcap antics are right out of *A Day at the Races*. In her Munchkin voice, she'll affect a Liverpudlian accent reminiscent of Tracey Ullman and do vintage Monty Python bits. But kidding aside, "I live to race," she says with as straight a face as she can muster.

That statement is confirmed by Krone's 1988 record of rid-

ing 1,958 mounts to purses totaling $7.7 million, respectable revenue for a small corporation. The four-foot-ten-inch, one-hundred-pound, Michigan-born horsewoman takes it all in stride, though the money is not easy to earn. She'll ride from five to nine mounts per day and get paid only forty-five dollars for races in which she doesn't win, place, or show. And the pace is frenetic. Between races she has all of seven minutes to get off a horse, scamper to her dressing room, and, with a valet's help, change into other silks, while scraping assorted ordure from her face. It's no life for the squeamish.

Her off-track bedding for now is at a simple two-story wood-frame rental she recently took with Jerry Casciano, an accomplished photographer of the racing scene in general and Julie in particular. Another important person in Krone's galloping lifestyle is manager Larry "Snake" Cooper, whom she dubs "just about my best friend."

Krone's affinity with fauna extends to her two cats, Scaggs and Slinky, who race into the living room from around the clubhouse, turn, and leap up onto the desk for a photo finish. They coexist peaceably with Krone's lovebird, in a house already filling up with many plants and fresh flowers. The desk, she confesses, was just moved in, mostly for our benefit, since she conducts most of the business side of her business from a copy

of the day's *Racing Form* and a pay phone at the track.

Easy, golden-oldies rock plays in the background, boxes of yet unpacked books—fiction, horsemanship volumes—and an easel displaying a jockey painting of hers give evidence of her many other interests. But riding and racing are clearly way out in front.

It took young Julie Krone nine years of hustle and travail, including a broken back, to attain her current catbird seat. The dozens of awards and trophies she's accumulated mostly reside in trunks that are rarely unpacked, given her nomadic life. One of the few on display is the glass bowl next to her—a gift for winning the 1988 Maryland "Lassie" Race—which serves as a convenient receptacle for her *Racing Form* and riding whip. Nearby is a Norman Rockwell statue of a jockey, *Weighing In*, and a Tiffany clock awarded for "Leading Jockey 1988 Meadowlands." A cordless telephone attests to her moving-about motif, as does the large carved penguin under her desk, "liberated" from a display at nearby JFK Airport.

Over the desk is a treasured photo of a dangerous moment in the 1962 Kentucky Derby, an appropriate collectible for a woman (born the next year) who takes serious chances every day to win her kingdom on a horse.

JAY LENO

While many of Leno's contemporaries engage in assembly-line humor, he hones his refreshingly empathic material in his garage.

One thought emerges about Jay Leno: His popularity isn't based on one-liners, profanity, racial stereotyping, or assembly-line humor but on the simple ups and downs of everyday life, which he weaves into a headline-fresh comedic tapestry.

Leno, thirty-eight, is not one to cast himself as a Greek chorus observing the world from the sidelines. Celebrity or not, he's as susceptible to the same neuroses as any of us. He is so much at home with the people in his audience for the simple reason that he is one of them.

There is, however, one indulgence that Leno has allowed himself, out of his relentless passion for anything automotive. A lifelong love affair with cars and motorcycles is evident once you step into his garage and meet the extended Leno "family": a '55 Buick Roadmaster, a '54 Jaguar XJ120, a Lamborghini Espada, two Lamborghini Miuras, a Lamborghini Countach, a three-wheeled Morgan, an M & L Cobra, a Bentley Turbo, and a nineteen-motorcycle collection comprising mostly antique Vincents and Harley-Davidsons.

Leno is so at ease in his garage that he parks his desk there. Strange? Certainly not to the comedian's wife, writer Mavis Nicholson Leno, who was elated that her handy husband finally moved the thing out of their study and into the garage. She would no longer have to explain to guests that the clunky steel sculpture atop Jay's desk wasn't a David Smith original but the remains of a twelve-cylinder Lamborghini's cracked engine block he could not bear to throw out. Nor would she have to continually justify magazine cutouts of the sexy sports cars that graced the study wall. "I'm not one of those guys who put art up on the walls and stare at it. My art is strictly kinetic and can be driven."

Leno was raised in the Boston suburb of Andover, the son of an Italian insurance executive and a charming Scotswoman. After college, he worked as a mechanic at a Rolls-Royce dealership, and at night he haunted Manhattan comedy clubs, constantly fine-tuning his comedic material as one would a racing engine.

Today Leno enjoys a career that is split between guest hosting the *Tonight Show* and giving more than 250 performances around the country each year. Because the themes he embraces and the human weaknesses he gently satirizes touch every audience, he is committed to playing the small venues— from Council Bluffs, Iowa, and Anchorage, Alaska, to Pocatello, Idaho, and Hanover, New Hampshire—even though he sells out Carnegie Hall, Caesars Palace in Las Vegas, Harrah's in Lake Tahoe and Reno, and The Sands in Atlantic City.

Leno is not at his Beverly Hills home that often, but when he is there, his routine consists of slipping into his mechanic's overalls, heading for the garage, plopping down in an oversize green leather chair Mavis thought she had thrown out long ago, and poring through newspapers and magazines in search of *Tonight Show* monologue material.

For as long as people are able to laugh at their own folly and insecurities, Jay Leno—living by his wits—will be there to remind them of the humor in the world around them.

LARS-ERIC LINDBLAD

The intrepid Lindblad's Antarctic desk in the 70s was aboard the *Lindblad Explorer*.

KEITH SHACHLETON

If the huge inlaid-mahogany desk seems unusually empty of the sort of piled-up paperwork and global paraphernalia one would expect to find in the office of someone who has sent more Americans farther north and south and into more off-the-beaten-tourist-track places than anyone other than the President as Commander in Chief, it's probably because Lars-Eric Lindblad is seldom in his office. In 1988, the jovial and gregarious sixty-two-year-old Swedish-born travel pioneer and founder of Lindblad Travel of Westport, Connecticut, spent an aggregate of eight weeks in the office; the year before, no more than six.

The rest of the time, Lindblad is off somewhere, armed with one of his 35mm cameras and portable typewriters, scouting new "adventure tours" for his curious clientele, revisiting his favorite venues—East Africa and

Antarctica—or challenging frontiers long closed by the political exigencies of various cold and hot wars. For example, it was Lindblad as much as President Richard M. Nixon who "opened up" mainland China, by bringing in the very first American tourists, later introducing them to Tibet, and then pioneering luxury cruises on the Yangtze River. More recently, he took advantage of Mikhail Gorbachev's *Perestroika*, persuading the Kremlin to let Lindblad Travel's camera-laden customers ply the Lena River in deepest Siberia.

"The old 'safe and sound' travel destinations are no longer attractive to the curious traveler," insists Lindblad, who got into the travel trade with Thos. Cook & Sons in Europe and founded his own firm in 1958 in New York after working for American Express. "People want to see, do, and learn about parts

of the world they have only read about." Accordingly, each year Lindblad Travel books some two hundred "learning adventure tours," lasting anywhere from thirteen to twenty-two days, for about eight thousand affluent Americans at an untouristy $3,500 to $7,000 a head.

Comparatively sparse though Lindblad's office is, what's there leaves little doubt as to the occupant's trade. The walls are hung with sundry travel trade certificates, awards, and citations, as well as photos of milestone events in the history of Lindblad Travel; the shelves hold various pieces of native soapstone and wooden sculpture; family photos and snapshots taken abroad; and plaques, including one obviously given him by his staff: *Rule #1: The Boss is Always Right. Rule #2: If the Boss is Wrong, See Rule #1.* On the desk are sheets of Kodachrome transparencies, the stuff of which Lindblad's handsome brochures are made; three whale teeth (which he is quick to say were pressed upon him by some Eskimos unaware of Washington's endangered-species list of proscribed items); a gold ingot from South Africa (a fake, given him in recognition of the first "wing safari"); an onyx desk clock from Hong Kong; souvenir boxes from Vi-

enna's Imperial Hotel (a favorite urban "watering hole" of Lindblad's); and a photo of him and his third wife, Ruriko, in the Falkland Islands.

What sets Lars-Eric Lindblad apart from other packagers is his role as travel educator and ardent conservationist. On each trip, escorts include specialists in such disciplines as Egyptology (Nile cruises), ornithology (the Galápagos Islands), Sinology (China and Mongolia), etc. Given his lifelong interest in exploration, matched only by his deep-seated concerns over what increased group travel might do to indigenous ecologies, it was only logical that Lindblad Travel became the first in the industry to commission or lease specially configured ships that would keep groups small and lessen damage to the virgin environment. When he was inducted into the American Society of Travel Agents' Hall of Fame, ASTA proclaimed Lindblad a latter-day Marco Polo, an adventurer-explorer with a conscience. Similarly, his efforts earned him an appointment as Special Adviser to the United Nations on Wildlife and Nature Conservation.

JOHN MADDEN

A *rolling* desk? Rolltop, you mean? No, his desk is built into a $450,000 custom-equipped Greyhound bus, the "MaddenCruiser."

It's all because of his legendary fear of flying that John Madden, pro football's gregarious commentator, TV pitchman, and progenitor of the "All-Madden Team," takes his work onto the bus and leaves the driving to one of Greyhound Corporation's finest. Most autumn Thursdays, a Greyhound driver rolls the "Madden-Cruiser" up to Madden's West Side residence in Manhattan and takes on his passenger, whom he deposits many hours later at the site of his next CBS-TV game, where Madden works alongside play-by-play announcer Pat Summerall.

At each refueling stop, every 750 miles, Madden wanders off for a vigorous, mind-cleansing walk—his only chance for daily physical workouts when on the road. On board, he mostly stays behind the desk, researching and preparing himself for the Sunday game.

The desk doubles as a dining table and in many ways resembles the sort of blond Formica tabletops one sees in Amtrak's buffet cars. Upholstered plaid seats are built in on both sides. The bus is equipped with a cellular phone and a CB radio, which enable Madden to broadcast his daily radio show from the highway.

The telephone is attached to the beige-brown wall at Madden's right, just above a set of videotapes he keeps handy in preparation for the next game. TV and VCR control devices are also within reach.

Madden is a voracious reader, and his desk is usually strewn with newspapers and magazines. On his way to Dallas for the Cowboys–Redskins game, he thumbs through the *Washington Post*, a Redskins press guide, newspaper clippings, and information sheets from both teams. Gifted with keen memory skills, Madden does little note-taking but keeps a small pack of flip cards nearby. Some of them contain the names of his nominees for the All-Madden Team, composed of hard-nosed, blue-collar types who play football the way Madden likes it.

The desk is also adorned with a rotator for the TV antenna, marker pens, and a copy of Madden's latest book, *One Size Doesn't Fit All*, written during his first year on the bus.

Madden has a glass of liquid protein on his desk, along with a bagel, sometimes smeared with (gasp) peanut butter, which he likes to wash down with Mountain Valley water from Arkansas. The bus is equipped with a well-stocked galley, a full-sized rear bedroom, and toilet/shower facilities.

Preparation done at this vagabond work station has paid dividends for CBS, especially in terms of the electronic video "chalkboards" technique that Madden pioneered. The recent addition of a backward/forward control on these instructional instant replays has increased efficiency to a point where Madden could explain play-action passes to an extraterrestrial.

Further evidence of Madden's professional acumen was noted in the Minnesota/San Francisco first-round playoff game on New Year's Day, 1989. With time running out in the first half, the Vikings punted and the 49ers called for a fair catch at midfield, whereupon Madden correctly predicted to the incredulous TV audience that the 49ers were entitled to a free kick for a field goal—a play commonly associated with rugby but almost never seen in American football.

That sort of on-the-job excellence has been the hallmark of Madden's career. In 1969, at age thirty-three, he became the youngest head coach in pro football. Ten years later, after considerable success, he resigned and later moved into broadcasting. Further career changes should not be ruled out for this freewheeling savant, who (like Jack Kerouac) has always believed in the importance of staying on the road.

J. W. MARRIOTT, JR.

Marriott's on-the-road desks are in each of the 460 Marriott hotels around the world.

If there's one thing J. W. Marriott, Jr., never worries about, it's forgetting his office address. Only, as he tells it, the modern office building at Marriott Drive in suburban Bethesda, Maryland, is his "second office." His *real* office is his well-scuffed and burnished leather attaché case, which he carries aloft some 200,000 air miles a year to Marriott hotel rooms around the globe. The company is one of the largest employers in the United States—460 hotels, 2,400-plus institutional food and services management accounts; in-flight catering for more than 150 airlines; Host food, beverage, and merchandise operations at 52 airports; and over 1,000 fast-food, family, and turnpike restaurants. Bill Marriott, fifty-seven, the company's chairman, needs to spend an inordinate amount of time "on the road" to make sure that the company,

widely recognized as one of the best managed in America, continues to stay on top.

Like all Marriott desks, the one in Marriott's office is polished to a fine sheen. It holds an ornate antique receptacle (containing paper clips), decorated with two entwined golden serpents; a matching lamp; and a Tiffany quartz clock recessed in an engraved wooden box. Nearby is a marble pen and pencil set bearing the inscription: *It's the 25th Anniversary of Your Department*. These objects, plus a plain black telephone, a desk blotter, and orderly sheaves of paper, are the most you, and probably he, will ever see on the chairman's desk.

Don't be fooled by the formal demeanor, though. Marriott loves to rev up fast sports cars, and he isn't averse to appearing as himself in various TV and print commercials to promote the Marriott name and product—for *USA Today*, in a Hathaway shirt ad sporting an eye patch, and pitching AT&T telephone cards to phone users everywhere. When it's Marriott hotel ribbon-cutting time, he's usually the one with the scissors.

Even his staunchest rivals compliment Bill Marriott on his outstanding executive ability, which includes giving a careful ear to staffers—most of whom are company stockholders.

Sitting on Marriott's office

windowsill is a stuffed teddy bear with a bandaged paw; his staff hoped it would cheer him up while he recuperated from burns received in a powerboat accident. A plastic model of a grinning "Big Boy," the logo of a fast-food company Marriott operates, and a smaller one of "Pappy Parker," the symbol for a fried-chicken product developed for the Hot Shoppes twenty years ago, are on a credenza directly behind Marriott's desk. Flanking the desk are Old Glory and the Marriott standard, both daily reminders of the chairman's civic duty and corporate responsibility.

The art in his office includes *Night Rescue*, a maritime oil by Montague Dawson; three military paintings by John Marry; and *First Lifeguards*, a painting by H. de Daubraw.

Besides being a workaholic who regularly puts in a fifteen-hour day, the University of Utah graduate is a devoted family man, an active member of the Mormon Church, a director of the Chamber of Commerce of the United States, and a member of the national executive board of the Boy Scouts of America, as well as a trustee of the Woodrow Wilson International Center for Scholars, the Mayo Foundation, and the National Geographic Society.

WYNTON MARSALIS

Marsalis, possibly the finest jazz trumpet player today, is also a superb classical concert artist.

CBS RECORDS

Eight-time Grammy award-winner Wynton Marsalis, who doubles in brass as a virtuoso of jazz and classical music and is now considered to be the likeliest successor to Louis Armstrong's long-empty throne, does most of his cerebral work sitting down at his 88-key "desk"—which, like so many other musical instruments these days, was made in Japan. He, of course, was made in the cradle of jazz: New Orleans, U.S.A.

Those who have seen and heard Marsalis play, whether as a symphonic soloist at Carnegie Hall or as leader of the Wynton Marsalis Sextet at the Brooklyn Academy of Music and at numerous jazz venues, marvel at his dexterity, his discipline, his *cool* as a lyric trumpeter—so different from the extruded heat of Dizzy Gillespie or Maynard Ferguson and so reminiscent of the early Satchmo.

Marsalis was weaned on the musical scale, and although his father, noted jazz pianist and music theoretician Ellis Marsalis, made no dynastic demands on his offspring, Branford became a world-class tenor and soprano saxophonist, Delfayeo a renowned trombonist, and Jason a drummer. As for Wynton, he's recorded for CBS Masterworks most of the serious trumpet concerti—Haydn, Mozart, Handel, Fasch, Torelli, Telemann, Charpentier, Purcell, Gabrieli.

He went into classics for the same reason Sir Edmund Hillary climbed Mount Everest: because it was there. The simile is more than apt. Six years ago, Marsalis told Whitney Balliett, *The New Yorker*'s jazz critic, that he studied classical music "because so many Black musicians were scared of this big monster on the other side of the mountain." Having proved the mountain a hillock and the monster a pussy-cat, Marsalis spends much of his off time running inner-city musical workshops and underwriting scholarships that, he hopes, will expose more young people to the jazz idiom.

Meanwhile, at twenty-eight, he finds his personal metronome weighted more heavily toward jazz. It is Christmas in New York, in the Manhattan townhouse he shares with his fiancée, Candice Stanley, and their infant son, Wynton, Jr. He is clearly rhapsodic about a new jazz piece he is scoring.

On the mantelpiece above the piano is a framed photo of one of his idols, Edward Kennedy "Duke" Ellington. Nearby stand three novelty figurines—likenesses of Satchmo—gifts from singer Sarah Vaughan. Beside them is a Royal Welsh Fusiliers trumpet going back to the Indian raj, and on the floor—amid Wynton Junior's scattered toys—a snare drum and a basketball.

In consideration of his neighbors in the East Twenties, Marsalis doesn't blow the bugle, but he does dribble the ball every once in a while down the hardwood floor of the high-ceilinged room—"to break the tension," he says.

Also to make a point. "The whole proposition of motion is essential to both jazz and basketball," says the pedant's son. "I've never seen Michael Jordan make the same move twice. It's all improvisation, like jazz."

He is ardently in love with Lady Jazz and courts her with all the passion of a man who savors her infinite variety, fickleness, and unpredictability. Understandable: he's escaped from a milieu of orderliness, as repetitive and disciplined as a Bach fugue. Having spent the past thirteen years building the kind of public acclaim other professional musicians would cheerfully kill for, Wynton Marsalis is off on a new and riskier gig, rekindling an awareness of jazz as an art form and leading the march to the sounds of different drummers. And bass players. And pianists. And guitarists . . .

YOKO ONO

There's more to life than being John Lennon's widow, so Ono's heavy schedule now includes stoking her own flame while meticulously keeping his.

Rising from her swivel chair, a replication of King Tutankhamen's throne, Yoko Ono Lennon studies her "Box of Smile," an Ono-designed silver cube in which one's countenance is mirrored. From behind her ivory-inlaid, Egyptian-influenced mahogany desk in the spacious white-carpeted and cloud-ceilinged room she occupies on Manhattan's Upper West Side, she astutely manages her diverse agenda. There is Yoko the songwriter/poet, artist, photographer, philanthropist, and single parent to Sean, her teenage son. Then there's the *other* Yoko, the fifty-six-year-old widow of John Winston Ono Lennon, the most idolized rock musician of the twentieth century.

The room, part of a converted studio apartment John Lennon dubbed "Studio One" shortly after they moved to the Dakota in 1973, overlooks Central Park—and now Strawberry Fields, the landscaped enclave dedicated to the immortal Beatle. The huge desk is a fanciful, early-twentieth-century French representation of the Gate of Rendering Justice the pharaohs had built for themselves during the Old Kingdom's Fourth Dynasty, while its solar disks are reminiscent of the reign of Akhenaton of Dynasty XVIII. Lennon bought it in Paris in 1977, along with the Art Deco vase that reposes below the desk's pedestal.

"When John and I decided to exchange roles—he a house-husband—he said, 'This is my gift to you for starting your own business. Use it as a trash can.' Then he signed a blank check. I keep it here on my desk, uncashed and framed."

Other desk items are a Tiffany snail-shaped lamp bought at a Sotheby auction, an ivory letter opener, a crystal-clear ball, and a whimsical touch: an apothecary jar containing "Half a Wind," inspired by Lennon and Ono's first "joint venture," a London art show similarly named. "We are all halves; the other half you don't see," Lennon said, then asked, "Why not put the other half-wind into a jar?" She did.

An adept touch typist, Ono composes lyrics and poems on her black IBM Selectric. The Art Deco statue in the background suggests, she says, "I'm independent. I'm free." The statue and a *faux*-tropical tree are juxtaposed against a smoked-glass mirror—"which is not meant to reflect but to see another world." This is clearly *her* space: open, serenely lit, and predominantly white—"the color of purity and honesty," she explains.

The Western-educated daughter of a Japanese banker, Ono met Lennon in London in 1967 and married him two years later. Now, as his widow, she finds within these oak-wainscoted walls the spiritual solace and energy she needs to preserve Lennon's professional and artistic legacy.

With a successful one-woman show at New York's Whitney Museum behind her, she has put her own artistic career on semi-hold in order to resume her chosen profession, as "keeper of the wishing well." Over the past nine years, she had produced three record albums of her own—*Season of Glass*, *It's Alright*, and *Starpeace*—a book of photographs, and a "very personal" video of her and Lennon. Now, she says, she wants to get back to meeting a long-standing commitment: "I had promised the fans that every year, until his fiftieth birthday, I would bring out something of John's."

Thus, last year she produced the 103-minute, $7-million David Wolper theatrical film biography, *Imagine: John Lennon*, a sound-track album, and *Imagine*, a sumptuous Macmillan coffee-table book. The phenomenal box-office success of the documentary, narrated by Lennon himself over material distilled from over two hundred hours of newsreel footage, home movies, still photos, and TV interviews, established beyond a doubt that the magic of Lennon now touches millions too young to have heard him during his brief lifetime.

Aided by her staff, Ono oversees myriad nonprofit trusts and foundations that have allowed her to expand her philanthropic horizons beyond the issues of nuclear disarmament and world peace, into such new causes as the homeless and other unfortunates who are bearing the brunt of government funding cutbacks—"in apology as a member of the human race and in the hope of world peace."

Petersen's drive for quality makes Ford second to none in profitability.

Quality is Job 1.

At the Ford Motor Company, where "Quality is Job 1," Job 1 belongs to Donald E. Petersen. The chairman and CEO, since 1985, of the second-largest car company in the world has helped transform it into the *most* profitable car company in the world. From losses at the rate of $1 billion a year in the early 80s, Petersen's inspired leadership enabled Ford to record almost $6 billion in profits in 1988.

After forty years filling key product-planning and development roles in many divisions throughout the far-flung Ford world, the tall, trim, sixty-three-year-old Petersen surveys, from his twelfth-floor executive suite atop Ford's world headquarters in Dearborn, Michigan, what he and his quality commitment hath wrought. His forty-foot windowed wall oversees Ford's gigantic Rouge Manufacturing Complex (a major armaments plant during World War II, now producing Mustangs), its R and D center and test track, and, farther away, the Henry Ford Museum and Greenfield Village.

An early riser, the former U.S. Marine (two hitches—

World War II and Korea) is up at six, arrives at his office by seven for a workout on his exercycle, followed by a shower and breakfast. Though he's at his desk by eight, he usually waits an hour to make phone calls. (Earlier in his Ford career, it was SOP to have meetings at seven and to get calls then, too. He vowed that if he ever had the power to do otherwise, he would.) The large, handsome, dark teak pedestal desk was designed by and custom built for Henry Ford II, last of the Ford family occupants of the executive suite. Displayed on its hard, highly polished top are the *Wall Street Journal*, the *Detroit Free Press*, the *New York Times, USA Today, Barrons*, and *Ward's Auto World*. Next to the publications sits a small stack of current nonfiction and business books. Petersen, an avid reader, makes time for writers like Tuchman, Manchester, and Wouk. Much of his daily intelligence comes via the large RCA Dimentia monitor-receiver to his left, with its conventional channels plus the company's own closed-circuit news network, beamed to more than 250 Ford facilities to

keep all of them in touch with the quality push. Piles of videocassettes update the chairman on new product design and development.

Petersen can get the right time from the complicated-looking Mensa clock on his desk (he's a member of that high-IQ society) or from the petite French antique eight-day clock next to it. The international map-clock on the teak credenza behind his desk chair provides an instant fix on worldwide Ford facility times. Adjacent to that is the master schedule of meetings and events Petersen must attend. "There's too much mail and meetings," he says in a rare grumble. Dotting the surfaces of his work areas are several of his favorite things, scale models of innovative cars he nurtured and helped develop: the futuristic Probe V, the Taurus, and the Sierra, among many others. A control panel next to a watercolor painting of vintage Fords enables Petersen, a serious jazz enthusiast, to trigger a state-of-the-art sound system.

Petersen is also a word buff, as an opened, well-thumbed unabridged *Random House*

Dictionary on the credenza attests. Next to it are framed family photos featuring his wife of forty-one years, Jo Anne ("Jody"), his son, Donald Leonard, and his daughter, Leslie Carolyn, and shots of himself with Henry Ford II and other Ford executives. Commanding the visitor's eye in this richly carpeted, elegantly furnished suite is Petersen's minerals collection. A large, lighted glass cabinet stands near the door, with shelves of his stunning specimens. Along the walls and adjacent to his desk are other showcases of remarkable stones. It all started about twenty-five years ago, when Jody gave him a gift of a quartz specimen; it bloomed into a major family obsession, which they avidly pursue in their world travels. An adjunct to his fascination with minerals is the gleaming brass balance scale on his desk.

What does he drive? one wonders. Actually, a variety of company products, including a Taurus, a European-built Ford Sierra Cosworth, and the Lincoln Mark VII LSC (Luxury Sport Coupe).

Petersen is clearly a man of enthusiasms—for cars, for driving, for his family and his company. His talent is the ability to communicate his enthusiasms and motivate the 350,000 people worldwide who constitute the Ford Motor Company.

FROM THE DESK OF:

ANDRÉ PREVIN

"Wave the stick until the music stops; when the music stops, then turn around and bow."

EVAN WILCOX

"A symphony conductor's desk," observes André Previn, the guest conductor of the Los Angeles Philharmonic and principal conductor of London's Royal Philharmonic, "is usually not terribly important to him. We do our work either at home, studying, or out there—on the podium."

Home to Previn depends on where you find him. For about fourteen weeks a year, between September and May, it's in Los Angeles, where he achieved much of his early fame as an Oscar-winning film composer at M-G-M and as an accomplished jazz pianist before embarking on a full-time symphonic career in 1960.

By the time Previn became the Los Angeles Philharmonic's ninth conductor, in 1985, he had been music director of three major symphony orchestras: Houston (1967–69), London (1968–79), and Pittsburgh (1976–84).

When Previn is not guest-conducting the Los Angeles, Vienna, or Berlin Philharmonic, he, his wife, Heather, and his five-year-old son, Lukas, are at their twenty-acre estate in Surrey, England. "There," says Previn, "I have a *real* desk, an antique stand-up desk that I adore and which I had to go to the ends of the world to find. I love it, because when I compose, I stand."

But in his backstage office at the Dorothy Chandler Pavilion in Los Angeles, Previn does a lot of sitting behind a gilt-edged, leather-topped, polished mahogany Regency-style desk. "When Heather first saw this backstage room, she thought it needed a few 'touches,' so she got this desk, leather chair, and a couch," he explains.

His view of the job of music director here is best summed up by a framed cartoon—one of many poking fun at his profession that hang in his office—showing a want-ad sign placed upon a music stand labeled *L.A. Symphony*. It reads:

HELP WANTED
Resident Orchestra Conductor; Party Goer; Gladhander; Fundraiser; High Visibility; Some Knowledge of Music Desirable.

Another cartoon shows a conductor at the podium, reading instructions on the music stand:

Wave the stick until the music stops; when the music stops, then turn around and bow.

Atop the Baldwin upright piano, next to a stack of scores, are framed covers of a ski magazine featuring young Lukas. On the wall over the piano hang two impressionistic brown-and-gray crayon drawings of Previn conducting done by Previn's son Matthew, now a Yale sophomore, when he was eight.

A framed photo of Lukas sits on the desk, alongside a conductor-in-the-box toy given Previn a few years ago by his close friend Tom Stoppard, the British playwright, with whom he wrote the 1979 "music drama," *Every Good Boy Deserves Good Favour.*

"Tom came by one terrible day when I had to let someone go and I didn't know how to do it. Tom left, came back an hour later with this thing, out of which popped an orchestra conductor. He told me, 'Just put a note in his little hand, reading, "You're fired." Then have the fellow come in and hand it to him.' " Previn chuckles ruefully at the memory.

FROM THE DESK OF:

WILLIAM SAFIRE

At his *New York Times* desk, Safire's a favorite essayist and columnist. At home, he writes best-sellers.

"My chair may be in Syracuse, but my desk's in Washington," says slouchy, deceptively dour-looking *New York Times* Pulitzer Prize–winning political columnist and resident etymologist William Safire, referring to the $1 million endowed Chair in Modern Letters that was established in his name last year by college friends. His oak rolltop desk, manufactured circa 1910 in Grand Rapids, Michigan, cost considerably less, says his British-born wife, Helene, who found it in a London antique shop a few years ago. Having swapped his legendary "rapier-sharp pen" for an IBM desktop computer, Safire had the desk retrofitted to house the terminal and keyboard but made sure to keep the mail slots on the side. "This way," he says mischievously, "sources can still slip me notes when the rolltop's locked up for the night."

As befits one of the *Times*'s star columnists, Safire's weekday venue is a suite of offices that he shares with his secretary and researcher, across the hall from a similar setup occupied by James "Scotty" Reston. As his columns are generally regarded as the best-researched in the business, it may be strange to see the desk barren of notebooks and files. That's because he does his "work-ups" on a large worktable outside camera range, in a book-lined anteroom.

Safire has made the office more comfortable by bringing in from his Chevy Chase home some Regency antiques and such decorative accessories as the Frederic Remington sculpture and part of his extensive collection of antiquarian books—Poole's *English Parnassus*, Crabb's *Synonyms*, Maunder's *Scientific Literary Treasury*, and the *Life & Letters of Admiral Farragut*, a hero of his. His vast treasure trove of contemporary dictionaries, thesauri, and other word reference books lines most of the walls of this as well as the adjacent office, which otherwise are remarkably free of the sort of doodads and flotsam that work their way into most journalistic dens. The few exceptions: a big ceramic ashtray on top of the desk, which he "liberated" from a German bar during his Army tour in the 1950s; a candy dish brimming with pistachio nuts; and a few of his ebony, glass, wood, ivory, and porcelain miniature whales—which he insists "do not represent my moving targets."

In 1978, Syracuse University awarded him an honorary doctorate in humane letters to compensate for the fact that he never graduated when he should have (in 1951), instead becoming a "legman" at the now defunct *New York Herald Tribune*. After the Army and a stint as an NBC radio producer, he went into public relations. It was in that capacity that he first made his mark: At a 1956 Moscow trade fair, he somehow managed to inveigle wily Nikita Khrushchev into visiting the booth of Safire's home-builder client, where Vice-President Richard M. Nixon just happened to be. The resulting photo, taken by Safire, which shows a finger-waving Nixon lecturing the Soviet premier on the virtues of capitalism, was picked up around the globe; it cemented Nixon's image as a cold warrior and ultimately brought Safire to Washington. In 1968, the President-to-be hired him as the White House's "rhetorician-in-chief." During Nixon's first term, Safire produced such zingers and snappers as "nattering nabobs of negativism" and "hopeless, hysterical hypochondriacs of history." Not for nothing had he written *The New Language of Politics*, hailed as the most innovative work of its kind since H. L. Mencken's *The American Language*.

After quitting the White House, Safire wrote two books—the nonfiction *Before the Fall* and a political novel, *Full Disclosure*—and aroused journalistic ire and fire when the *Times* hired him as conservative counterweight to its stable of liberal columnists. Predictable but unflappable, he quickly built a reputation as an uncompromising advocate of free speech and scourge of Potomac pomposity and won himself the coveted Pulitzer Prize. His Sunday "On Language" column provokes an astonishing three hundred letters a week, more than any other regular *Times* column.

GEORGE SHEARING

Sid Lerner, Hal Drucker and associates are here this morning to
photograph my desk. I have a feeling, however, that we will never be in
the top ten.

George Shearing

George Shearing plays cards with a marked deck. He feels that's fair: The cards are in Braille. This brilliant, blind pianist is an intrepid punster. Not quite a master bridge player, Shearing is unquestionably master of the keyboard. A glance at his desktop tells you that mastery extends beyond the piano.

Atop Shearing's eight-drawer contemporary mahogany desk sits a showcase of modern technology: a VersaBraille word processor hooked into a Smith-Corona L-1000 printer, which turns out standard type text; a Maryland Computer Services Modified Brailler, which writes in Braille; and nearby, a "reading machine" (Xerox-Kurzweil Personal Reader), which stands ready to scan the book *America Observed*, by fellow Brit Alistair Cooke. This last robotic wonder reads aloud in any of nine voices and at a variety of speeds! Sharing the remaining desk space are the requisite answering machine, a normal AT&T telephone, and a Panasonic eight-line Easaphone speaker phone.

Flanking Shearing's center of command are, not unexpectedly, two teak Yamaha upright pianos along one wall, a variety of recording equipment and tape decks lining the other.

The many awards and memorabilia gracing the walls bear testimony to Shearing's long and illustrious career: photos of Leonard Bernstein and Michael Feinstein, an autographed picture of the late Boston Pops maestro Arthur Fiedler, a reprint of a *People* magazine article. The gallery includes White House invitations from three administrations and a cartoon from the magazine *Punch*, showing two American tourists in the Alps asking an Alpine longhorn player: "Do you know 'Lullaby of Birdland'?" Shearing, a veteran Birdland performer, is of course the composer of that world-famous tune.

It's here, in the office/den of the New York apartment that he shares with his wife, Ellie, that Shearing tinkers with his electronic toys and his music. "There's an album coming out which I just made with Hank Jones; we ran through some stuff up here for that album," Shearing declares. "But I don't work very hard anymore; it's going to be my seventieth birthday coming up." Not working hard to Shearing's mind translates as full speed ahead to anyone else's. At present, he's arranging a Dixieland album, playing a two-shows-a-night engagement at the Café Carlyle (a twelve-block walk from his home), and preparing for his annual tour with longtime fellow jazz aficionado Mel Tormé.

Shearing's love affair with jazz and piano has been a never-ending gig of playing, composing, arranging. It started back at Linden Lodge, the school for the blind Shearing attended as a youth in England. After a year playing at a pub following graduation, he joined Claude Bampton's All-Blind Band, through which he met Leonard Feather, a jazz legend and mentor, who arranged engagements for Shearing in the States. The rest, as the pundits and Shearing fans will tell you, is history.

But the Cockney coalman's son from Battersea has never forgotten the lessons of being a "less fortunate"; he plays with Mel Tormé for a different charity every year. On the "nuisance" of being blind: "I was instrumental in getting the area codes put in Braille by AT&T, as well as the peripheral consumer information," says Shearing. "What I really want is to have as much material accessible to the blind—in Braille—as there is available to the sighted at the same price. It's not fair to pass the additional cost of Braille books on to the blind."

An embroidered pillow on a nearby couch in the office sums it up: "Life is like a piano; what you get out of it depends on how you play it." No one has a better feel for life—or that instrument—than George Shearing. For a man who has had to write his own script, he's made some beautiful music.

GAIL SHEEHY

With the soul of an outdoorswoman trapped in the body of a workaholic writer, Sheehy types wearing gloves and mukluks at her almost-outdoor desk.

"Normally, I would feel like a shut-in when I'm writing, because I love the outdoors," says Gail Sheehy, standing in her nestlike twelve-by-twelve-foot office, nine floors above Fifth Avenue on the glass-enclosed terrace of her "working" apartment. "Here I feel like I'm outside even when I'm inside."

Outside is an incomparable view of Central Park and Manhattan's Upper West Side. On the terrace are potted rose-bushes, laurels, pines, and a birch tree, which spring to life during warm weather. (There is also a circular trampoline, on which the trim, five-foot-three-inch author goes into her Flying Wallenda routine mornings at 5:00 A.M., when she's working on overdrive and needs to discharge the extra energy.) "To be able to watch when thunderstorms start and the wind begins swirling is a wonderful thing,"

she explains. "I couldn't live in Manhattan and be a writer any other way."

Sheehy's airy office contains reminders of her accomplishments: two of her four Front Page awards from the Newswomen's Club of New York, whose symbol is Pegasus; cassettes of her numerous interviews—"I just came back from London, where I did forty in two weeks"—and a 1979 Harvard Graduate School of Business award recognizing her as an "Outstanding Human Behaviorist, Author, Journalist." There is also a telephone, a Sharp fax machine, and a white Formica kneehole desk, which holds research materials and books.

At her busiest, Sheehy clocks in twelve-hour days on an IBM PC word processor at her four-by-five-foot easel desk. In winter, when even a baseboard space heater and standing portable radiator don't keep her

warm out on the terrace, she wears mukluks—"I got them on a writing assignment that sent me to western Alaska"—and gloves (which don't inhibit her ability to type) to keep going. Spring and summer are a different story. "Central Park is my front yard," she says, "and when the weather is warm, I spend two hours a day having lunch on a park bench, reading, and watching the pigeon feeders."

On the window ledge over her easel is a framed invitation showing Sheehy standing next to a life-size, die-cut picture of President Reagan, with a bird perched on his head. The caption reads: "Tina Brown invites you to the celebration of the publication of Gail Sheehy's newest book. . . ." Next to this is an in-box of research files for an article she is writing on Margaret Thatcher, a small quartz clock, ten or so reference books, and a framed photograph of "all my favorite people"— Sheehy with her sister, husband, Clay Felker, editor of *Manhattan, inc.*, and daughters Maura and Mohm.

There is also a large, opened *Webster's Third International Dictionary* ("I always like to use a new word in every article"), an elegant photograph of Sheehy and Felker taken in one of England's Great Houses during their recent trip, and floral-printed tin boxes containing

desk accessories and supplies. On her desk is a large bronze statue of a mythical nude female warrior astride a flying horse (recalling the Newswomen's Club symbol), a 1987 Christmas present from her husband, who gave it to her as "a spur."

"The Shoeleather Sheehy Award," a gag gift given to her by *Vanity Fair* political editor Elise O'Shaughnessy, consists of a pair of women's shoes entirely covered with magazine articles Sheehy wrote for the publication about the 1989 presidential candidates. "I went to every one of their hometowns"—she laughs—"and *did* real shoe-leather reporting."

The author of eight books— including *Character: America's Search for Leadership* and *Passages*, which was on the *New York Times* best-seller list for three years—Sheehy is the contributing political editor for *Vanity Fair*, often writes for *The New York Times Magazine* and *Parade*, among others, and appears regularly on such programs as *Nightline*, the *MacNeil Lehrer NewsHour*, and *Good Morning America*.

Even so, she has a hidden goal not everybody knows.

"I love the theater," she admits, "and my secret dream is to write a play."

NEIL SIMON

Rumors is flying, like all of Simon's Broadway comedies since *Come Blow Your Horn*, his first.

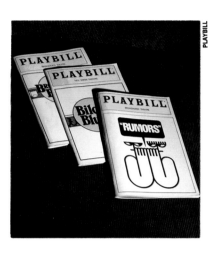

PLAYBILL

The partners desk in the well-postered *California Suite*–like study in Neil Simon's ranch-style house in the Hollywood Hills obviously makes a most practical writing surface—if Simon only wrote longhand, which he doesn't: witness the Adler typewriter. But it's a great storage area. What is impractical, admits Broadway's most prolific writer of comedies, is a set of false drawers on each of the sides.

No matter, you'll find Simon working both sides. The print version of Simon, seen on the cover of *Ranch & Coast*, a San Diego lifestyle monthly, is parked atop the partners stool, front row center. The flesh-and-blood Simon, dressed "Bel Air Casual" (sneakers without socks, tailored sports clothes), is seated in the rear. Missing is the *legitimate* Neil Simon, the Broadway theater on West Fifty-second Street he purchased a number

of years ago with proceeds from his hits (though, curiously, his own plays never run there).

On the back wall, framing this latter-day Yankee Doodle Dandy—Simon, like George M. Cohan, was born on the fourth of July (in 1927)—are posters featuring six of his past efforts: *Barefoot in the Park*, *The Star-Spangled Girl*, *Come Blow Your Horn*, *Sweet Charity*, *Little Me*, and *The Odd Couple*.

This workingman's desk, Simon's first, was bought in the late 50s. Here (or at his downtown office) the prolific bard of comedy favors a tufted swivel-back chair, with a cushion for an occasionally ailing back. A disciplined writer, he is at his desk by nine each morning, toiling until midafternoon. "It's the only way you can get it done. I don't worry about whether I'm getting it right or not, I just try and get it out. If I get the general idea, I can always rewrite. I

used to think three pages a day, fifteen pages a week, maybe a play in six or seven weeks. But it generally doesn't work out that way."

On the desk itself is an odd-lot collection basking in the wattage of a top-heavy Chinese-vase-turned-lamp: baseball figurines; a miniature *Playbill* from *Broadway Bound*, the last play in his semi-autobiographical trilogy, which was preceded by *Brighton Beach Memoirs* and *Biloxi Blues*; a glass sculpture engraved with the final couplet from Shakespeare's twenty-ninth sonnet: "For thy sweet love remembered such wealth brings/ That then I scorn to change my state with kings." It is flanked by a dime bank (Simon was a boy during the Great Depression). The thrice-married father of two daughters is an adoring grandpa; there's a favorite photo of Simon bussing his only grandson. Behind the tool of his trade, the mighty Adler, sits another cherished memento, a hand-inscribed game ball from the San Francisco 49ers' Bill Walsh, 1989 Super Bowl–winning coach, Simon's good friend and regular tennis partner.

Simon's early muse turned pro at Tamiment, a Catskills-like resort in Pennsylvania's Poconos, which over the years proved a hotbed for nurturing creative talents. He worked there with his brother Danny for two years following a stint in the Air Force. Here Simon also met the counselor in a nearby

girls' camp who became his first wife. "We worked really hard: 10 revues over the summer, and the pay was twenty dollars a week." Revue producer and mentor Max Liebman helped the brothers Simon make the jump from Borscht Belt to Broadway. As producer of TV's *Your Show of Shows*, he hired the two to write for Sid Caesar (other notable Caesarian scribes were Mel Brooks and Woody Allen). The job lasted four years.

Well before the two Tony Awards and the name above the marquee, it began, not in Brighton Beach, but in Washington Heights, the old neighborhood that helped feed and nurture his career. "I miss the Automats up in the Heights. I remember standing there with a pad in hand, jotting down things about the people who would sit there for hours scooping out the baked beans with pieces of bacon or pork from those little brown jugs, or the change-makers who would flick out nickels with their fingers with the aplomb of a Paderewski. Fascinating!"

He saw his first play, Richard Wright's *Native Son*, right in the neighborhood; he was stunned. "I knew I wanted to be a writer but it wasn't until I saw this drama and, shortly after, my first Broadway musical comedy that it hit me. I told my parents, 'I could do that.'"

Although not one to blow his own horn . . . he did.

FROM THE DESK OF:

DON SIMPSON AND JERRY BRUCKHEIMER

B & S believe in sharing—a 20-foot desk at Paramount and $1.7 billion at the box office.

In Hollywood, where offices are more than just offices and furnishings as much a clue to status as notches on a Polynesian totem pole, the office of Simpson/Bruckheimer Productions is bound to confound.

Occupying all of Cecil B. DeMille's old headquarters on the Paramount lot, just off the rococo gate immortalized by Gloria Swanson (as Norma Desmond) in Brackett and Wilder's *Sunset Boulevard*, the office of forty-three-year-old Don Simpson and forty-five-year-old Jerry Bruckheimer belies their importance as the hottest ticket in Tinseltown. Four of their films—*Flashdance*, *Top Gun*, and *Beverly Hills Cop I* and *II*—have generated over $1.7 billion in theatrical, record, and VCR sales. Just one of the films (*Top Gun*) has made each a centimillionaire.

What's more, they have ac-complished this without leaving in their wake a trail of the sort of fear and loathing that can make visits to the producer's office an exercise in unholy terror. The environment may have much to do with this anomaly.

In their cavernous high-ceilinged office, you will not sink up to your ankles in white plush rugs. As a relatively new team—they got together in 1983—they lack the sort of "junkman" inferiority complexes that led such studio tyrants as Louis B. Mayer and Harry Cohn to turn their desks into raised thrones. The black leather sofas are for conferencing, not for eager starlets to "audition" their way to stardom. "We're just too damned busy to play around on our time," says Simpson, a native Alaskan who started out as a Warner Bros. gofer and ended up at Paramount, as production president, making such hits as *Urban Cowboy*, *48 Hours*, and

An Officer and a Gentleman. Fifteen-hour days are common for the team once they're "in production."

Indeed, in a town where it's de rigueur to lure production chiefs with $100,000 "office decoration allowances," this place could pass as a mahogany-paneled, green-walled pit stop between soundstages.

Take away the framed celebrity photographs (George Bush, et al.) that adorn both sides of the divider separating the partners' respective work areas; forget about the original Warhols, Keifers, and Motherwells on the walls; pay no mind to the rosewood humidor filled with cigars fit for visiting tycoons (neither partner smokes; both of them are health freaks)—and what you're left with is a hangar-like room in which someone mistakenly parked a huge twenty-foot-long table along with six Charles Eames leather-and-chrome swivel chairs.

But it's no mistake: this is the way Hollywood's Dynamic Duo like to work—equal but separate. From such studied indifference to ostentatiously displayed power has sprung a perpetual geyser of ideas and income to boggle the mind. And they clearly have fun doing their thing.

"We don't have to impress anybody anymore," says buttoned-up, businesslike Bruckheimer, the quieter of the two,

who favors dressing the part of a studio executive—unlike the more voluble Simpson, who prefers blue jeans, black shirts, and cowboy boots.

The two couldn't be more dissimilar, not just physically but also in the way they work and in what piles up: Simpson collects—magazines, scripts, tapes, cans of film, correspondence, any scrap of paper that might contain the germ of an idea for their next film; while Bruckheimer—a neat and orderly pile-maker—disposes.

Voracious readers both, they subscribe to nearly a hundred publications. "I do my trade-magazine reading at home. Here I take care of the details," says Simpson, who elaborates: "In war, I'd kill the enemy in hand-to-hand combat. Jerry would do it from the bunker, using electronic equipment." Bruckheimer doesn't disagree. "We're like different parts of the same brain," he says.

That might explain why, despite their contradictory personalities, both had the interiors of their homes designed by Don Umemoto and why, until recently, they drove matching black Ferraris. Even their secretaries are identical twins, which sometimes confuses the staff but not their employers.

STUDS TERKEL

Pinned to the corkboard wall over the "organically disheveled" desk at Chicago's radio station WFMT is a *New Yorker* magazine cartoon depicting a wife about to answer the phone, while her husband, seated nearby, says: "If that's Studs Terkel, there are seven or eight things I'd like to get off my chest."

The endearingly compassionate seventy-seven-year-old cigar-chomping Terkel, America's foremost oral historian and self-confessed "bleeding heart liberal," explains: "If you have a cartoon in *The New Yorker*, that means you've arrived."

Actually, Louis "Studs" Terkel—who drew his nickname from the protagonist of James T. Farrell's "Studs Lonigan" trilogy (for reasons he will not reveal)—"arrived" long before he won the 1985 nonfiction Pulitzer Prize for *The Good War: An Oral History of World War II.*

Standing out in any crowd by virtue of his invariable red-checked shirts, red ties, and red socks—"Make that *Garibaldi* red, please"—Terkel has been a hometown celebrity since the late 1940s, when, for three TV seasons, he played the genial barkeep of a Chicago saloon on *Studs' Place*, one of the first network sitcoms.

His rumpled demeanor and midwestern vibrato cast him as the logical successor to Carl Sandburg as the Windy City's poet laureate. More than two decades later, he would be tapped as midwest commentator-at-large on PBS's *The Great American Dream Machine*, and more recently, he appeared in the film *Eight Men Out* as a fictional Chicago sportswriter who helped expose the 1919 Black Sox scandal.

For the past thirty-six years, he has hosted the hour-long wheeling *Studs Terkel Show* weekdays on Chicago's WFMT (which lists him on its personnel talent roster as "Free Spirit"). It is now syndicated nationally.

Although he has a law degree from the University of Chicago, he's never practiced. Graduating during the Depression, he instead became a professional dabbler—federal civil service worker in New Deal Washington, radio soap opera actor ("I always played the gangster who'd say, 'OK, boss' "), playwright, jazz columnist, disc jockey, panel moderator, lecturer, film narrator, music festival host, sportscaster, and, of course, oral historian.

He's always been the consummate listener, letting other people talk, treating every word—every pause—as revealing. Whether writing or just conversing on the air, Terkel describes what he does as "gold prospecting—mining a lot of ore-grade stuff, which I then spend hours sifting and cutting to get to the gold dust."

His demonstrable knack for extracting from long conversations kernels of insight that historians tend to dismiss as chaff prompted Pantheon's André Schiffrin to propose that he do a book on American "village life." The result was *Division Street: Chicago* (1965), the first of Terkel's many oral histories. He "went national" five years later, with *Hard Times: An Oral History of the Great Depression.* His eighth book, *The Great Divide: Second Thoughts on the American Dream*, was published in 1988.

Terkel works out of a hopelessly cluttered, book-lined office at WFMT. His is not so much a desk as a work station in such a permanent state of disarray that his secretary now leaves his mail on his swivel chair, lest it disappear into the paper quicksand. Reels and cassettes abound, as do piles of books on chairs, the sofa, and the floor. He persists in hunting and pecking on an old manual Remington and pretty much resists the tyranny of electronic gadgetry. Thus he still watches an ancient black-and-white Magnavox TV (under the desk) but has caved in partially by abandoning his trusty but klutzy shoulder-hung Uher tape recorder in favor of a miniature Sony palm-sized unit ("I've gone from one defeated World War II enemy to another") and installing an air-filter device to remove the lingering bitter odor of his daily cigars.

The push-pin board contains the usual working clips, research, cartoons, and famous sayings so beloved of writers. There are photos of some of the people he's admired: his boyhood idol, socialist Eugene V. Debs; jazz pianist Thomas "Fats" Waller; blues singer Bessie Smith; and *chanteuse* Edith Piaf. Also displayed is a clip from the *Oak Ridge* (Tenn.) *Journal* headlining Hiroshima, and an extract from *The Great Gatsby* about the Buchanans ("They were careless people [who] smashed up things").

BARBARA WALTERS

Walters's 1977 interviews with Sadat and Begin were among her favorites.

One of the first things to catch the eye as one walks into the Lincoln Square office of Barbara Walters—ABC News's top-rated, globe-trotting, headline-making TV journalist—is the rose-colored pillow on the settee, embroidered with the words: "I really mean it this time. I'm going to slow down." Another eye-catcher is her Olympia manual typewriter. One is tempted to take neither seriously. Barbara Walters slowing down? Walters, the nonpareil electronic journalist, pecking away on a *manual?*

Don't be so sure about the latter. At one point, she gets up from her comfortable chair and wordlessly crosses the office to do by hand what others do by the flick of a button. Surrounded and probably suffused by the network's state-of-the-art electronics—monitors, speakers, zapping devices—Walters ac-

tually *walks* over to a TV set concealed behind mirrored doors and deftly flicks the channel selector. Great wrist action. The incongruity of it all! Here is TV's reigning superstar doing things the way they used to do them in the dark ages B.C.—Before Carson. Dare we say that Barbara Walters isn't remotely interested in remote controls—or in such fundamental labor-saving devices as the electric typewriter? She does not disagree.

As for slowing down, she says, "Don't be silly. After thirty years in the business, I wouldn't know how." Actually, she was born into show biz, when it was more "show" than "business." Her father, Lou Walters, was the famous Latin Quarter nightclub impresario and an intimate friend of many stars. It explains why his daughter is so unfazed in the company of celebrities.

Her pace requires that she

have not just one but *three* offices—two in New York, the third on the West Coast. Most of her time is spent in office number one, from where she operates as co-host with Hugh Downs of the weekly Friday-night *20/20* program. The second office, just a few blocks away in the sprawling ABC Television West Side Manhattan "campus," is where she works preparing her two-time (1981–82, 1982–83) Emmy Award–winning *Barbara Walters Special* celebrity interviews—which *Vanity Fair* says has displaced the *Time* magazine cover as "the ultimate accolade of stardom."

The third office is in Hollywood, convenient to the Bel Air home she shares with husband Merv Adelson, head of Lorimar Telepictures. (The Adelsons also maintain a co-op in Manhattan.)

Here in office number one, her working life revolves around the circular glass-topped desk, "fully loaded," as they say, with a ten-line ITT phone, the obligatory box of sharpened pencils and Magic Markers, scripts, pads, correspondence to sign, cassettes, coffee mug, and the day's marked-up newspapers.

Displayed on the wall near the window are Walters's favorite pictures and cartoons, among them a 1978 *Doonesbury* strip by Gary Trudeau, poking fun at her; another, by Tom Botniak, ribs her famous 1977 dual interview with Anwar el-Sadat and

Menachem Begin. Photos of Walters with the Egyptian and Israeli leaders, flanked by two pages of her interview notes, are also framed and hung, as are a *Life* magazine cover of her and autographed photos of Walters interviewing Fidel Castro, another of her scoops.

On the windowsill and shelves there are various Emmy and other industry awards, as well as tributes from the Anti-Defamation League of B'nai B'rith.

Neatly arranged on the bookshelves next to her desk are the indispensable reference books—*Webster's Thesaurus*, the *American Heritage Dictionary, Who's Who in America*—videotapes of past shows, notebooks filled during such historic trips as the 1972 visit of Nixon to China and the 1975 follow-up by President Ford, various celebrity books sent her by hopeful publicists, and the script for her landmark two-hour *50th Barbara Walters Special*, which aired in November 1988, reprising memorable interviews with such as the Shah of Iran, John Wayne, Bing Crosby, Katharine Hepburn, Bette Davis, Sir Laurence Olivier, and Barbra Streisand.

Things occasionally disappear from her offices, but one object never leaves her sight—her bulging appointment book. "If I lose this," she says, "my life is over."

JOHN WEITZ

"**A**ny man who uses his desk as a Maginot Line," asserts noted menswear designer John Weitz, "deserves what the Maginot Line got." In his 1974 book, *Man in Charge*, Weitz tore apart "the idea of one man behind a desk and another man in front of it, of bully and victim or ruler and subject." Seated in a corner of his coolly elegant twenty-fourth-floor midtown Manhattan office near the Plaza Hotel, the German-born, British-educated (St. Paul's School), sixty-six-year-old Weitz is unequivocal: "A desk should be a place to write papers, examine papers, store papers, *period*."

Rumor has it that Weitz's Teutonic certitude may have piqued Simon & Schuster editor-in-chief Michael Korda into adding to his Machiavellian spoof of success primer, *Power!*, the fiendish idea of positioning your desk against a window so that the sunlight streaming in will blind all supplicants and cow them into doing your bidding. Not the Maginot but the Siegfried Line.

The tall (six-foot-one-inch), trim, and patrician Weitz has no patience for such games. *His* desk—actually a non-intimidating thirty-two-by-forty-eight-inch white Formica-topped artist's easel—is wedged into a back corner and faces a wall of organized clutter; thus he is forced to swivel around to communicate with licensees and staff of John Weitz, Inc., his $250 million design company, giving them his full and undivided attention.

He clearly draws comfort from the montage facing him: photos of his wife, actress Susan Kohner, their two sons, and family friends; production shots of the X600 sports car he designed; jackets of books he has written; Christmas cards; art exhibit fliers; cartoons and blow-ups of quotations he likes ("John Weitz contends that people wear their sportscars. Therefore the sportscar *is* a part of fashion"). What Korda calls "power tools" are, to Weitz, just that: tools of the design trade: T-square, triangle, oversized shears, rubber cement, trade magazines, portable electric typewriter—all else is stored out of sight in a movable, multi-drawered utility cabinet by his side. He clearly uses the desk for what it was meant to be—an exceedingly functional *work* space.

Described by one admiring magazine writer as "the kind of man every other man imagines himself to be: devilishly handsome, sartorially resplendent and very successful," John Weitz is indeed, to some degree, all of the above. At one time, film producer Albert "Cubby" Broccoli even approached him as a possible successor to actor Sean Connery as James (007) Bond, but Weitz turned him down, laughing. "I had already done the *real* thing"—an allusion to his World War II stint with the Office of Strategic Services, the forerunner of the Central Intelligence Agency.

An all-business blue suit at the office and Yankee pinstripes on the field make Winfield Topps in any league.

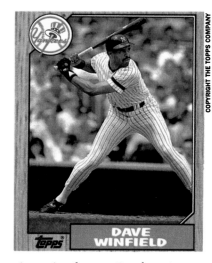

COPYRIGHT THE TOPPS COMPANY

DAVE WINFIELD

Topps

"**W**infield, you're one helluva ball player, and you've got *class!*" Of all the honors showered on the famous New York Yankees outfielder—or "infamous" if your name happens to be Steinbrenner—none means more to Dave Winfield than Pete Sheehy's offhand compliment. Until his death a few years ago, Sheehy was the Yankees clubhouse attendant, going back all the way to the days of Babe Ruth.

An autographed photo of Sheehy sits on the windowsill behind Winfield's desk at the Fort Lee, New Jersey, headquarters of the David M. Winfield Foundation, the organization he founded over a decade ago to help less fortunate kids become productive members of society. The desk, with its modern silver pedestal supporting a black Formica top, is well suited to the six-foot-six-inch multimillion-

aire, who favors *Gentlemen's Quarterly* apparel appropriate to corporate board rooms.

Winfield, who grew up in a single-parent family in St. Paul, went on to win Big Ten championships in baseball and basketball and became the only man ever to be drafted in three professional sports: the National Football League's Minnesota Vikings, the National Basketball Association's Atlanta Hawks, and the National Baseball League's San Diego Padres. Like Jackie Joyner-Kersee, Winfield believes "professional sports have given me the opportunity and the forum to help those who are willing to help themselves."

The sill also holds photos of Winfield's wife, Tonya, an executive with Xerox Corporation, and his daughter, Lauren Shanel. There is a picture of "Winnie" being greeted in the Oval Office

by President Ronald Reagan and Vice-President George Bush, and in another shot, Winfield, in the White House Rose Garden, receives a plaque from Reagan for providing jobs for youth. There is also a portrait of the 1988 American League All-Star team, as well as a framed cartoon that appeared soon after Winfield's highly successful 1988 memoir, *A Player's Life*: in a jam-packed bookstore, one happy clerk asks another: "Are there any more books that George Steinbrenner doesn't like?"

Much of the book is devoted to family life, personal stories, and baseball. It also describes the foundation he developed on the principles that were important to the success in his life: health and education through sports. At first, Winfield awarded scholarships in St. Paul, and then, during his 1973–80 tenure with the San Diego Padres, he began designating part of his salary for thousands of grandstand seats to be offered to needy kids. He credits the original idea to Al Frohman, a Los Angeles–based businessman who served as a surrogate father as well as agent to Winfield.

The foundation's most recent campaign is called *Turn It Around*. It emphasizes positive group action as it does battle with drug abuse. A poster for the campaign is displayed near Winfield's desk.

Evidence that the man is in charge can be found in a gold

turtle-shaped desk bell, acquired on a trip to Toledo, Spain; he playfully taps it to signal to long-winded guests that it's time to head to the "clubhouse." A leather portfolio, which holds his most recent correspondence, was picked up on a trip to Argentina. Winfield's passion for travel can also be seen in a Seiko clock of the world's time zones.

Signs of "jockdom" include a Louisville Slugger bat representing "what I do best," and a memento of his Keystone Kops arrest by Toronto authorities in 1986 for killing a seagull while playing catch in the outfield. A ceramic gull with a baseball embedded in its side commemorates the incident. Also present is a Tiffany baseball, which is not embedded in anything.

Winfield keeps a Zenith AM/FM cassette player nearby. The radio dial is tuned to relaxing instrumentals, and the cassettes range from Sade and Ben E. King to subliminal motivational messages, which, he says, help him to focus his brain on the tasks at hand.

The mental concentration that results has been sufficient to make him the first player since Joe DiMaggio to drive in over a hundred runs for six consecutive years. Election to the Hall of Fame in Cooperstown is all but inevitable, the proper cap to a career that gained the approval of the man who saw all the great ones—Pete Sheehy.